CRISIS AND PREDATION

CRISIS and PREDATION

RESEARCH UNIT FOR POLITICAL ECONOMY

India, COVID-19, and Global Finance

MONTHLY REVIEW PRESS

New York

Library of Congress Cataloging-in-Publication Data
available from the publisher

ISBN 978-1-58367-924-1 paper
ISBN 978-1-58367-925-8 cloth
ISBN 978-1-58367-926-5 eBook trade
ISBN 978-1-58367-927-2 eBook institution

Typeset in Minion Pro and Univers LT

MONTHLY REVIEW PRESS, NEW YORK
monthlyreview.org

5 4 3 2 1

Contents

Preface

This writing began as a series of blog posts, trying to explain a basic, yet little-discussed, aspect of recent developments.

India's COVID-19 lockdown has been perhaps the world's harshest, imposed on an overwhelmingly informal workforce—and thus affecting the vast majority of the Indian people. Yet the Indian government's efforts to cushion this shock have been the paltriest in the world. Inevitably, the scale of distress has been staggering. What prevents the government from spending more?

Economists have variously ascribed this to the government's ignorance of economics, its faith in false financial dogmas, or its plain callousness. While all these explanations contain an element of truth, we believe a different reason lies at the root.

Global finance, which exercises a tight grip on India's economy, sets severe limits on the government's outlays. As we all know, the consequent broad-based collapse of economic activity has devastated millions of people. But what is less discussed is that this very drought in government spending is yielding a rich harvest for certain predatory interests—global financial investors and a handful of India's biggest business houses (in which foreign investors also hold large stakes).

Monthly Review Press is a publisher whose aims we identify with profoundly, so when it approached us about converting our notes into a book, we agreed immediately. We hope that, like so many other Monthly Review Press books, this one too will serve the needs of those struggling for fundamental change.

—RAJANI X DESAI FOR RUPE, OCTOBER 2020

1

The Choice Posed Once More by the COVID-19 Crisis

CONTINUING SUBORDINATION TO GLOBAL FINANCE, OR TAKING
A COURSE OF DEMOCRATIC NATIONAL DEVELOPMENT

Summary

This text makes the following points:

1. Even before the advent of COVID-19, India's economy was in a depression. The condition of vast masses of people, particularly those in the informal sector, was grave.
2. In its response to COVID-19, the Indian government imposed the most stringent lockdown measures in the world. Given the character of India's economy, this had a particularly severe impact on the majority of people.
3. At the same time, the government has barely spent to cushion the impact of these measures on people. Compared to other governments in the world, the Indian government has provided some of the lowest additional spending (as a percentage of gross domestic product [GDP]). While some further expenditures may be

forthcoming in the coming months, it is already clear that the final sum will be abysmally low. The actual fiscal expansion may come to around 1 percent of GDP for the fiscal year ending in March 2021, compared to 3 percent of GDP after the Great Financial Crisis of 2007–09. Of course, the crisis in the real economy now is much, much greater than that after the Great Financial Crisis.

4. This extraordinary tight-fistedness stems from the underlying fact that global financial interests explicitly oppose any sizable expansion of government spending by India, for reasons outlined in this book. Global finance is in a position to dictate this because Indian governments of all hues have, over the years, made the country dependent on flows of foreign capital. India's foreign exchange reserves, while seemingly ample, have been built up through funds from foreign borrowings and volatile foreign investments. *Given this dependence*, India's rulers abjure any sizable expansion of government spending. They fear that such an expansion would precede a downgrade by U.S.-based credit ratings agencies, an exit of foreign investments, a stock market crash, and a fall in the rupee's value. Thus, Indian policymakers are set on a course of attracting and retaining foreign capital inflows, even when there are large surplus inflows of capital.

5. In response to the present crisis, the government is faced with a choice. In theory, it could defy the pressure of global finance and address the basic needs of its people (an objective that is otherwise within the reach of India's present material capacity). This would, however, require imposing controls on destabilizing flows of foreign capital and being prepared to forgo such foreign capital flows in the future, and all that this implies, in order to pursue a course of democratic national development. For that, the rulers would need what they inherently lack given their very class basis— namely, a positive vision of democratic national development and a class alliance to bring it about. The other option is to submit to the regime of foreign finance, awaiting signals on how much they can spend at different junctures, giving up any pretense of economic sovereignty.

6. India's rulers have adhered to the latter course. Now, anxious to shore up the country's foreign exchange holdings and reassure foreign investors of their credentials, they are trying to attract foreign investments in government debt, with potentially grave consequences. The rulers have also appealed to the United States for help in addressing the foreign exchange crisis through the provision of "swap lines." If the United States were to extend such help, it would require a *quid pro quo* in the form of more complete subordination. Whether or not these investments and aid materialize, the country is being rendered even more vulnerable to volatile flows, thereby setting the stage for further crises and arm twisting.

7. The international economic and political crisis has been accentuated with the advent of COVID-19. The United States and its allies have used the emergence of COVID-19 to target China for reasons that have nothing to do with the virus. The present international crisis has also seen India's rulers draw even closer to the United States, integrating India into the strategy of the global hegemon. This has greatly aggravated unresolved disputes and tensions between India and China, setting in motion a border clash that will have far-reaching negative consequences for the Indian people, while serving U.S. interests.

8. The present withholding of government spending in the face of an unprecedented depression is resulting in enormous hardship, which in turn may result in unrest and upsurges. The rulers' actions against political opponents and activists of people's movements have been preemptive, punitive, and severe. As the situation unfolds, the prevailing emergency conditions allow for the more wanton use of repressive and divisive methods—such as reliance on security forces, state surveillance, detention of political activists and democratic persons, heightened communal propaganda, and censorship of independent media—in the name of controlling the pandemic.

These conditions pose more urgently than ever the choice outlined previously: whether to be resigned to the further subordination of the Indian economy and people's lives to global finance, or to take the path of democratic national development.

2

The Crisis before COVID-19

The present economic calamity has overshadowed the state of affairs that preceded COVID-19. But to even understand the present situation, we need to take stock of the immediate past.

In 2017–18, government surveys revealed a dire economic situation. The following two years, 2019–20, showed even further deterioration. These matters are usually discussed in an abstract way, as relating to something called "the economy," but it is important to see them as people's lives. We will look at employment, poverty, wages, and consumption, touching on the state of industry and investment along the way, as these indicate the state of employment and future prospects.

Suppressed Surveys

In January 2019, the National Statistical Commission (NSC) cleared the release of the 2017–18 *Periodic Labour Force Survey (PLFS)*. However, the government intervened to prevent its release until after the 2020 election, because it revealed an appalling situation: not only had unemployment levels risen to historic highs, in percentage terms, but even *the absolute number of persons employed had fallen* for the first time in the history of the government's statistical body's employment measurement.[1]

Shortly thereafter, the government decided to suppress the results of the 2017–18 *Household Consumer Expenditure in India (HCE)* report, despite it being cleared for release by a working group in June 2019 and despite the chairman of the NSC arguing for its release.[2] The survey shows that, for the first time in more than four decades of official measurement, *per capita consumer spending fell* in real terms (that is, after adjusting for inflation) since the previous survey.

The results of these two surveys confirm each other. As employment shrank, so did consumption expenditure. If you do not have work, you spend less, even on food.

Crisis of Employment

Well before the advent of COVID-19, India faced a grave crisis of employment, one that has worsened dramatically over the last few years. For decades, the percentage of India's employed population (known as the worker population ratio) was about 40 to 42 percent, a low figure compared to the rest of the world. This was the figure in 2004–05, but it fell steeply afterward. By 2017–18, it was just *34.7 percent*. (See chart 2.1, below)

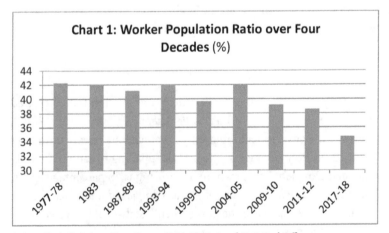

Source: *Periodic Labour Force Survey 2017–18*, National Statistical Office.

Had the worker population ratio remained the same in 2017–18 as it was in 2004–05, perhaps 95 million more people would have been employed (assuming the country's population in 2017–18 was around 1,300 million).

From the chart, we can see that a dramatic drop took place between 2011–12 and 2017–18. As mentioned, not only did the percentage of employed people fall, but even the absolute numbers of those employed fell. Estimates of the absolute reduction in employment vary between 6.1 million and 15.5 million.[3]

Youth Unemployment

The gravity of the situation can be seen in the following figures from a study by Santosh Mehrotra and Jajati Parida.[4]

- In 2017–18, the youth population (those aged between 15 and 29) was roughly 368 million. Of these, just 116 million were employed in any way.
- Another 25 million were in "open unemployment," that is, they were actively looking for work but remained unemployed.
- However, the figure of open unemployment is just the tip of the iceberg: *another 100 million youth were neither employed, nor in education or training.* They were "discouraged workers," who presumably had given up on looking for work or knew there was no use trying.
- Finally, 127 million youth were in education or training, spending their families' meagre resources and their own energies in the hopes of getting decent jobs after they completed their studies. Where will they go? These soon-to-be-graduates account for more than the total of all youth presently employed.

Growth of Poverty

The government eventually released the 2017–18 *PLFS*, even as it tried to discredit its findings. But it never released the 2017–18 *HCE*

TABLE 2.1: Where Are India's Youth (Ages 15–29)?

	millions
YOUTH IN THE LABOUR FORCE	
Employed	115.7
Openly Unemployed	25.0
YOUTH OUTSIDE THE LABOUR FORCE	
In Education/Training	127.0
Not in the Labour Force, Education/Training	100.2

Source: Santosh Mehrotra and Jajati K. Parida, "India's Employment Crisis: Rising Education Levels and Falling Non-Agricultural Job Growth" (working paper, Centre for Sustainable Employment, Azim Premji University, Bengaluru, India, October 2019.)

report, perhaps because it would have had even wider implications. Official consumer expenditure surveys are the basis for calculating poverty levels. Not only would it be deeply embarrassing for the government to admit that poverty had risen under its rule, but all government schemes targeting the "poor" would have had to be given additional funding.

We know that the official measurement of poverty in India has become an increasingly unreal bureaucratic-academic exercise that grossly understates poverty. But even using official definitions and methods, the data reported in the 2017–18 *HCE* report implied a sharp rise in poverty in the period between 2011–12 (the period of the preceding survey) and 2017–18. S. Subramanian, an expert in the field, finds that, even by the official methodology, the share of people living below the poverty line would have jumped by 4 percentage points. In absolute numbers, 76 million more people would have fallen below the official poverty line, amounting to a 20 percent rise in the number of officially "poor" people.[5] The government thought it better to scrap the survey itself (and may have succeeded in censoring the truth for a long time were it not for a determined journalist, Somesh Jha of the *Business Standard*).

Further Deterioration Post-2018

This record unemployment and growing poverty are not, in our view, a creation solely of the Bharatiya Janata Party-led government. They have roots in the underlying political economy of India, the policies of successive governments, and the bubble-led rapid growth of the period from 2003 to 2008.

Nevertheless, the policies of the Bharatiya Janata Party-led government—in particular the demonetization policy implemented in December 2016 and the goods and services tax implemented in July 2017—have greatly aggravated the crisis. These measures not only depressed employment and demand at the onset, but their second-order effects also further depressed employment and demand over time.

Depressed Agrarian Sector

India's agrarian sector was grievously hit not only by a global decline in agricultural commodity prices, but also by the domestic demand depression.[6] Terms of trade for agriculture (the index of prices received for farm products divided by the index of costs of cultivators) tell us whether cultivators' net incomes are improving or getting squeezed on the market over time. Terms of trade for agriculture in India have declined in the post-2010 period of fiscal tightening, meaning that land-owning peasants have been further impoverished through market processes.

The condition of rural laborers is even more alarming. Real wages—wages after taking inflation into account—tell us what and how much can be purchased with earnings. The real wages of agricultural laborers and other rural laborers started falling in March 2019 and continued to do so until January 2020, the last month for which we have figures. By January 2020, the real wages of these laborers were roughly *7 percent lower* than a year earlier. Since these laborers are at the lowest economic rung of Indian society, a 7 percent reduction in their real wages betokens a silent social calamity.

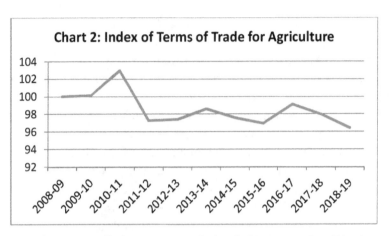

Index of prices received by farmers as a ratio of index of cultivation costs. Base: Triennium ending 2011–12 = 100. Source: *Agricultural Statistics at a Glance 2019* (New Delhi: Ministry of Agriculture and Farmers' Welfare, Government of India, 2019).

It should be noted that the wage rate for rural casual labor hardly increased between 2011–12 and 2017–18 according to the *PLFS*.[7] In the period after 2018, real wages actually fell.

Moreover, wage rates are only part of the picture. Incomes are the product of wage rates and days of employment. Total employment in rural areas shrank sharply between 2011–12 and 2017–18. The workforce participation rate fell by nearly 5 percent: in 2011–12, nearly 40 percent of the rural population was employed, but by 2017–18, it fell to 35 percent. We do not have data for the more recent period, but the situation appears to have worsened.

One sign of the deteriorating rural employment situation in the period after the release of the 2017–18 *PLFS* is the desperation of rural households seeking work under the Mahatma Gandhi National Rural Employment Guarantee Scheme (MGNREGS) over the last two years. In 2018–19, the demand for work increased by almost 10 percent compared to the previous year.[8] From 52.7 million in 2018–19, the number of households seeking employment under the scheme jumped to 54.7 million in 2019–20.[9]

This was despite the fact that *real wages under the scheme stagnated*

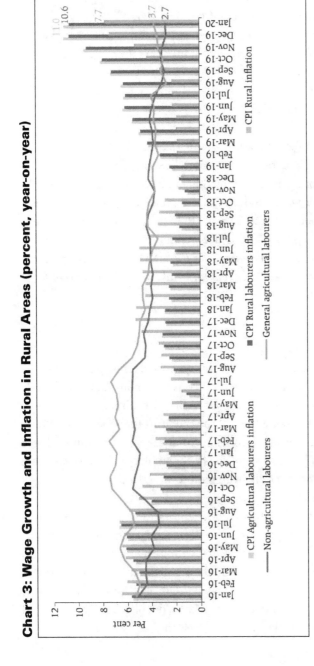

Chart 3: Wage Growth and Inflation in Rural Areas (percent, year-on-year)

Source: Reserve Bank of India, *Monetary Policy Report April 2020* (Mumbai: Reserve Bank of India, 2020).

for years at low levels and fell 6 percent in 2019–20.[10] Significantly, the government adopted a policy of keeping MGNREGS wages low in order to keep overall wages low, benefitting employers. That workers flocked to the scheme in increasing numbers despite the abysmally low wages shows the extent of desperation for employment. The Reserve Bank of India (RBI), India's central bank, is brutally frank about the state of MGNREGA:

> Moreover, in recent years, the Mahatma Gandhi National Rural Employment Guarantee Act (MGNREGA) scheme does not seem to support rural income much due to delayed wage payments, lower wages and insufficient budgetary allocations. The Periodic Labour Force Survey (PLFS) report released by the NSO [National Statistical Office] in May 2019 shows that *wages under MGNREGA work are lower than the market wage rate for non-public work by 74 per cent for rural men and 21 per cent for rural women.*[11]

Cutting Back on Consumption

Against this background of systemic demand depression, it is not surprising that rural consumption of "consumer non-durables" (largely ordinary items of mass consumption) shrank beginning in September 2019. Around the same time, corporate firms too reported that sales of fast-moving consumer goods in rural areas had plummeted to a seven-year low.[12] Purchases of consumer durables dropped even more sharply than non-durables, with motorcycle sales down 22 percent by February 2020.

This is confirmed by stark ground reports from rural areas. Sayantan Bera reports of villagers who rarely consume even legumes, surviving on *rotis* and salt, or rice boiled with turmeric and salt; mothers who are unable to give their children vegetables, fruit, or milk; and a manmade drought of employment.[13] Official data indicate that the number of suicides by daily wage earners doubled between 2014 and 2018, and has risen even further thereafter.[14]

At the same time, rather than ensuring the distribution of foodgrain to the hungry, the government hoarded it. Thus, foodgrain stocks reached 77 million tons in March 2020, whereas the April 1 foodgrain buffer stock norm for the central pool was only 21 million tons, meaning that the excess stock was 56 million tons.[15] On top of this, a good *rabi* (winter crop) harvest was anticipated in April, which was expected to add at least another 20 million tons to the stock.

Industry and Urban Areas in the Grip of Demand Crisis

Urban informal labor also suffered massive blows due to the recession: an eleven-part report from mid–2019, covering eleven cities (Delhi, Indore, Jaipur, Perumbavoor, Ahmedabad, Kolkata, Lucknow, Bengaluru, Bathinda, Haryana, and Pune), exposed a tale of employment devastation.[16] Unemployment and low wages in turn depressed demand for mass consumption goods. In the fourth quarter (January–March 2020), the volume of sales of fast-moving consumer goods giant Hindustan Unilever shrank 7 percent, indicating that sales had collapsed even before the lockdown began on March 24.[17]

Industrial growth, as measured by the Index of Industrial Production, fell by 0.8 percent in 2019–20 (in which there was only

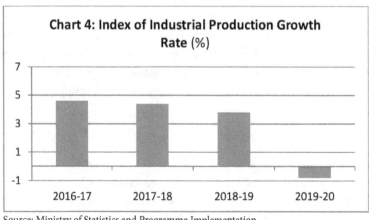

Source: Ministry of Statistics and Programme Implementation.

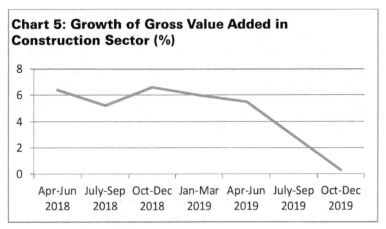

Chart 5: Growth of Gross Value Added in Construction Sector (%)

Source: National Statistical Office.

one week of lockdown). Electricity production slumped in the second half of 2019–20 due to lack of demand. The steep decline in construction activities had a particularly wide impact on the economy given that construction is a very large employer, accounting for 54.3 million jobs in 2017–18—almost as much as the entire manufacturing sector.

Even goods and services catering to the middle and upper classes saw a steep slump, as seen in the decline in launches and sales of new housing units, sales of automobiles (down 18 percent in 2019–20), and the performance of civil aviation.

By February 2020, the production of capital goods—a key indicator of the state of industrial investment in the economy—had fallen year-on-year for fourteen straight months. Indeed, it is not surprising that industry was not interested in investment: demand was so low that factories were running at only 69 percent of capacity.

Financial Sector Activities Increasingly Divorced from Productive Ends

In these conditions, such economic growth came less and less from sectors of material production, such as agriculture, mining, industry, utilities, and construction. These sectors contributed just 0.9 percent of the 3.9 percent of the official GDP growth estimate for 2019–20.

Chart 6: Construction Indicators

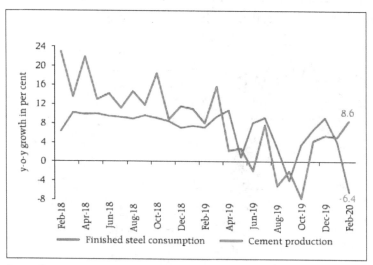

Source: Reserve Bank of India, *Monetary Policy Report April 2020.*

Chart 7: Passenger Transport Indicators

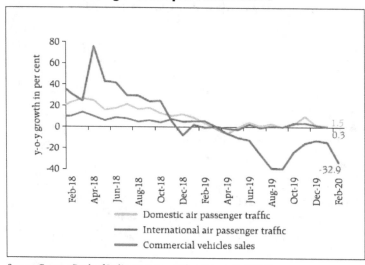

Source: Reserve Bank of India, *Monetary Policy Report April 2020.*

Charts 8a and 8b: The State of Investment Demand

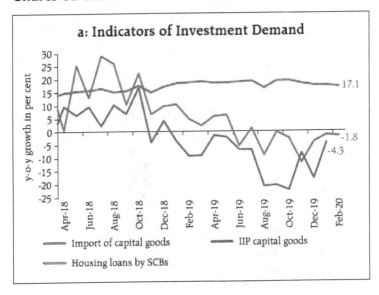

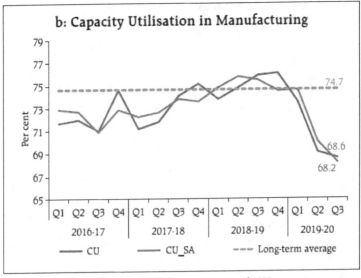

Source: Reserve Bank of India, *Monetary Policy Report April 2020.*

The remaining 3 percent came from three areas: (1) trade, hotels, transport, and communications; (2) finance, real estate, and professional services; and (3) public administration, defense, and other services. Finance, real estate, and professional services contributed more than a quarter of GDP growth, despite it being in a slump compared to its glory years.[18]

What was the financial sector doing in 2019–20? Bank credit growth slumped to less than half its earlier level and turned away from production. With industrial growth near zero, major corporate firms turning to foreign loans, and a backlog of bad loans to the corporate sector, banks stopped lending to industry. In 2019–20, they channeled their funds into personal loans—that is, loans to individuals for consumption. By February 2020, personal loans accounted for 61 percent of credit flow, the service sector for 26 percent, agriculture for 10 percent, and industry for just 3 percent. Apart from this, banks preferred to park large sums with the RBI itself, preferring to earn low interest rates rather than risk lending to productive activities.

The corporate sector itself "has stopped investing into new capacities for all practical purposes," noted the Centre for Monitoring the Indian Economy. "In the year [that] ended [in] March 2019, net fixed assets of the Indian corporate sector grew by a meagre 5.3 per cent. In better times, net fixed assets grew by 16–17 per cent in a year and even peaked at 23 per cent in 2008–09. The sharp fall in net fixed assets growth is bound to have an impact on the ability of the corporate sector to increase employment."[19]

Instead, the Centre for Monitoring the Indian Economy remarked, the corporate sector devoted an increasing share of its funds to financial instruments (such as shares, debt instruments, and mutual funds), which grew at a much faster rate than its investments in productive assets. This share rose from 6 percent of all assets in the 1990s to 12 percent in 2014–15, 15 percent in 2017–18, and 18.5 percent in 2018–19. In the year 2017–18, the value of such investments in their books was ₹2.5 trillion.[20] Evidently, the corporate sector was unconvinced that any recovery was in the offing and preferred to keep its money in liquid assets.

Corporate Slump, Intensifying Depression of Demand

From 2016 to 2019, demonetization and the goods and services tax led to a crisis for the informal sector, but at first the corporate sector actually grew by grabbing market shares away from informal units. However, the loss of incomes in the informal sector steadily deepened the problem of demand in the Indian economy, which eventually hit the corporate sector as well. In turn, the corporate sector slump, combined with a government policy of winding down or selling off the public sector, led to a wave of retrenchments and job losses in the formal sector, driving demand further down in a vicious circle. Mahesh Vyas notes:

> BSNL has shed over 78,000 employees while MTNL has shed over 40,000. . . . 35,000 were reported to be laid off in the [information technology] sector and the count was expected to go up to 50,000. The automobile sector faces its biggest slowdown of recent times. Bosch announced that it would reduce headcount in India by over 10 per cent. Hero Motorcorp is also shedding manpower. And, newage enterprise Ola is reducing its workforce by 5–8 per cent. Even food delivery enterprises like Zomato, Swiggy and UberEats are facing new challenges as growth has slowed down. Uber has reportedly cut staff by 10–15 per cent. Future Group was reported to be shutting down 140 grocery stores after having grown rapidly till recently. Oyo plans to fire 1,200 in India. NBFCs [non-banking financial corporations], brokerage companies face their own challenges.
>
> Public sector banks are being merged, Air India and more are to be privatised. More jobs may be lost.[21]

Endemic Paucity of Demand: A Feature of India's Political Economy

What was the nature of the crisis before COVID-19? The current government would like to ascribe the crisis to global conditions, which were already depressed. The parliamentary opposition would like to ascribe it to the ruinous steps of the Narendra Modi government, such as demonetization and the "manner of implementation of the GST [goods and services tax]" (the opposition does not criticize the tax itself, since it was party to it).

Both explanations, while partly true, are incomplete. The Indian economy has an underlying problem of demand. With a longer perspective, one can question the notion that India's "normal" growth rate is 10, or 8, or even 6 percent, and that any deviation from this is abnormal. Instead, one could argue that the "special episodes" that need explanation are the spells of rapid growth.

Colonial rule crippled the Indian economy. From the start of the twentieth century to the transfer of power in 1947, the annual rate of per capita income growth was 0.1 percent, and per capita agricultural production was actually negative. The end of colonial rule and a rise in public investment with the five-year plans gave rise to a spell of growth.

However, there was continuity with the colonial period in some spheres. Land was not significantly redistributed, nor were rural debts cancelled, nor was the capital of foreign firms, native tycoons, and big merchants touched. Rather, the post-1947 rulers soon turned abroad for funds and stepped down the rate of public investment.

The profound contradictions in this growth process culminated in a slump and stagnation, which extended from the mid–1960s to the end of the '70s.

In the late 1970s, nearly all the leading economists weighed in with their analyses of the stagnation. The most penetrating analyses pointed to (1) the endemic paucity of demand, due to the low purchasing power of the masses, and (2) the widening income disparities, which led to a distorted structure of demand, with production increasingly skewed to luxury consumption. Resolving this problem would have required radical agrarian reform and a different pattern of industrial development, ensuring the expansion of demand, self-reliance, and full employment. But such a resolution was obstructed by the existing social order.

The rulers tried to sidestep these obstacles to growth rather than overcome them; the measures they adopted, however, exacted their own price. In the agrarian sphere, the government introduced new, capital-intensive technology in pockets of the country during the 1960s, which began generating grain surpluses for the rest of the country.

In the 1980s, the government began liberalizing industrial policy, foreign collaborations, and imports. India's industrial growth finally soared, but this rapid growth was accompanied by a rapid expansion of the trade deficit and external borrowings, collapsing with the external debt crisis of 1990–91. This crisis marked a significant turning point and was followed by a major opening up of India's economy to foreign capital.

The next sustained spell of rapid growth was during 2003–08, fueled by the global boom and capital inflows. India's corporate profitability was then among the highest in the world. This growth was concentrated in goods and services for the upper classes— apartments, cars, consumer durables, air travel, various high-end services—and infrastructure to cater to all these. As the Index of Industrial Production was revised to take into account the changing structure of Indian industry, consumer durables, consumed largely by the upper classes, rose from 5.4 percent of the index in 1994 to 12.8 percent in 2012. Meanwhile, consumer non-durables—largely items of mass consumption—shrank from 23.3 percent of the index to 15.3 percent over the same period. This rapid growth ended abruptly with the global financial crisis of 2007–09.

For a couple of years after the financial crisis, the government revived growth by expanding the fiscal deficit (government borrowings) and pumping bank lending to the corporate sector. But from 2011, as the government once again started to cut spending, growth steadily began to decelerate. It continued to do so for the following decade. Had we more credible methods of measuring GDP, we might find that, by January–March 2020, growth had fallen to zero or even below zero.

The sectoral nature of growth too has changed over the years. Whereas a poor country needs to expand its production of material commodities (in agriculture and industry) to meet people's basic needs, in India the service sector has grown most rapidly. Its share of GDP has risen from 30 percent in 1951 to 40 percent in 1986, 50 percent in 2001, and 60 percent in 2014. By 2014, the finance and real estate sector had swollen to 20 percent of GDP—in a country marked by the majority of people's desperate struggles to survive.

India's long growth slump before COVID-19, from 2011 to 2020, was thus not merely the product of some external event or some specific government misstep, though these might have contributed to it. Rather, it was the expression of fundamental contradictions in the country's underlying political economy.

It is in the context of this grave depression that COVID-19 and the nationwide lockdown took place. The vast masses of toiling people, already impoverished by the depression, were cutting back even on subsistence expenditure due to lack of income. They were in no condition to take the blows that followed.

3

The Impact of the Lockdown on India's Conditions

The Indian rulers' response to COVID-19 was to "lock down" the entire country for sixty-eight days (from March 25 to May 31, followed by lockdowns in containment zones). Indeed, this was extended: the lockdown has not been fully lifted at the time of writing (mid–August).

This is without historical parallel. It finds few comparisons globally, even in these pandemic times. *The New York Times* called India's lockdown "the largest and one of the most severe anywhere."[22] The lockdown has been backed by punitive measures, left to the imaginative coercion of provincial governments, local authorities, and police in different regions.

As Jean Dreze notes, the word *lockdown* does not capture what India has done: "it's more like a curfew, or an attempted curfew."[23] A staggering 114 million lost their jobs and livelihoods in April 2020.[24] Out of work with negligible savings after months of labor, millions tried to return to their villages, many of them walking hundreds of kilometers, some of them attacked by the police on the way. Those who were forced to stay back in the cities were trapped in slum rooms or tiny tenements, starving, many forced to line up for food handouts.

Agricultural supply chains were disrupted, agricultural markets stopped functioning, and cultivators suffered huge losses on perishable crops.[25] More than five hundred thousand trucks were reported to be stalled at state borders. All this, and many other aspects, are now well-known.

At the same time, the government spent next to nothing to ease the pain of the measures. On March 26, India's finance minister announced with much fanfare the Pradhan Mantri Gharib Kalyan Yojana (Prime Minister's Plan for the Welfare of the Poor). The plan was officially put at a meagre ₹1.7 trillion, or about 0.8 percent of GDP, but its actual scale was even lower. Almost half of what was labeled "expenditure" under the March 26 announcement consisted of window-dressing.[26] Further, the single most important relief in the package—three months of distributing additional foodgrains for free through the public distribution system—would actually cost the government nothing at all, since its godowns were groaning with 56 million tons of excess foodgrain stocks on April 1, 2020, and more grains were to be procured in April–May from the latest harvest. (Later, by June 1, food stocks indeed rose to an unprecedented 104 million tons, posing a grave storage problem.)

London's *Financial Times* noted: "While other countries have rolled out massive relief packages to cushion families and businesses from the economic shock of coronavirus, New Delhi has largely left the population to fend for itself as it frets about its own finances, already weakened by the previous two years of a protracted economic slowdown."[27]

It appears that India is a global leader *in inflicting policy-based pain on its citizens* in response to COVID-19. This is brought out in two charts.

Chart 1 was released by the International Labour Organization (ILO) in April 2020.[28] It shows the condition of informal workers under lockdown and other COVID-19 containment measures. The bubble representing India is at the top of the chart, showing that the share of informal workers in total employment is much higher in India than in the rest of the world. These are low-income workers without security or benefits, who will be worst hit by any lockdown. Not only that, but the size of the bubble shows that the absolute number of such workers in India is also the highest in the world. Furthermore, the bubble is to the far right of the chart, showing that India has implemented the most draconian lockdown in the world.

The ILO remarks:

> In India, with a share of almost 90 per cent of people working in the informal economy, about 400 million workers in the informal economy are at risk of falling deeper into poverty during the crisis. Current lockdown measures in India, which are at the high end of the University of Oxford's COVID-19 Government Response Stringency Index, have impacted these workers significantly, forcing many of them to return to rural areas.[29]

Chart 2 presents the picture of initial government responses to COVID-19, as of April 8, 2020. This repeats one measure from the previous chart (albeit here on the vertical axis), namely, the stringency of government response: India's response was the most draconian in the world. The horizontal axis in Chart 2 depicts the size of government fiscal measures, as a percentage of the GDP of each country. In other words, it measures how much different governments worldwide had increased their spending and taken a range of other fiscal measures in order to cushion the terrible impact of these containment measures on their citizens. The Indian government's measures were among the most miserly in the world, which is why India is to the left of chart 2.

Together, the two charts show that:

- in India, measures such as sweeping lockdowns without warning or preparation can have a particularly devastating impact, since nine-tenths of the workforce is informal; *yet*
- the government imposed the most draconian lockdown in the world; and

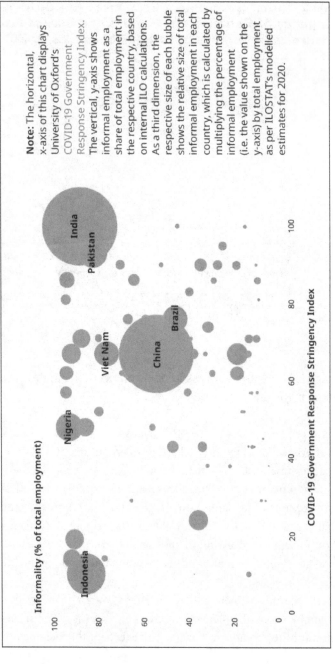

Chart 1: Informal Workers under Lockdown and Other Containment Measures

Note: The horizontal, x-axis of this chart displays University of Oxford's COVID-19 Government Response Stringency Index. The vertical, y-axis shows informal employment as a share of total employment in the respective country, based on internal ILO calculations. As a third dimension, the respective size of each bubble shows the relative size of total informal employment in each country, which is calculated by multiplying the percentage of informal employment (i.e. the value shown on the y-axis) by total employment as per ILOSTAT's modelled estimates for 2020.

Source: International Labor Organization.

Chart 2: Initial Government Responses to COVID-19—Stringency of Containment Policies and Size of Fiscal Measures as a Percent of GDP (as of April 8, 2020)

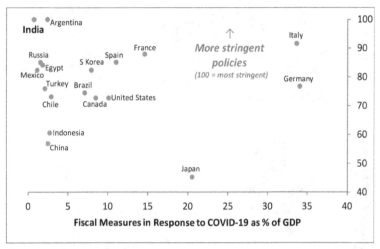

Sources: Oxford University COVID-19 Government Response Stringency Index; International Monetary Fund.[30]

- provided the least material succor or compensation in the world to those hit by these measures.

As a propaganda exercise, the government's March 26 package was utterly eclipsed by the package it rolled out from May 12 to 17. The government claimed that the May package brought the total stimulus to nearly ₹21 trillion. This claim was quickly debunked by over a dozen leading banks, brokerages, and credit ratings agencies, which put the actual fiscal stimulus in the region of ₹2 trillion—a ratio of window-dressing to substance of 10 to 1.[31] As such, the Indian government's economic package remained among the lowest in the world.

Thus, the government neither let people earn their livelihood, nor compensated them for their losses in earnings, nor sustained them until they could work again. The effects of the lockdown were predictable, yet the government hardly budged an inch to help those affected. N. K. Singh, Bharatiya Janata Party leader and chairman of the Fifteenth Finance Commission, proudly declared: "This current political leadership will not give in to the macroeconomic temptation for fiscal profligacy.... It is quite conscious of our vulnerabilities, and how these things can get out of hand. *Maintenance of macroeconomic stability must be the cardinal principle.*"[32]

The rulers' conception of "macroeconomic stability" appears to be compatible with the devastation of the vast majority of people's lives.

We will not go into the details of the devastation and suffering caused during the lockdown, as these have been widely reported. Our intention in presenting the two charts is simply to show that (1) the suffering could have been anticipated by anyone familiar with the structure of India's economy, and (2) it was not merely the handiwork of some lower-level functionaries, but the outcome of a thought-out policy of the government, pursuing its "cardinal principle" of "macroeconomic stability."

The central government enforced this "cardinal principle" on state governments as well. In India, well over half of all government spending and two-thirds of all developmental spending (that is, social services such as public health and education, and economic services such as irrigation) are carried out by state governments. Now, state governments also bear the overwhelming bulk of expenditure in relation to COVID-19, both in health care and general relief. Yet, their spending has been straitjacketed. They have been barred from borrowing more than 3 percent of GDP in "normal" times.

Despite the extremity of the present circumstances, the central government has relaxed this straitjacket on states' expenditure by only a paltry *2 percent* of GDP, and that too is hemmed in by various conditions. (Of this, only 0.5 percent is automatic. Further dribs and drabs will be tied to states' implementation of "reforms" demanded by the center: borrowing 1 percent of GDP will be allowed in four tranches of 0.25 percent, "with each tranche linked to clearly specified, measurable . . . reform actions," and an additional 0.5 percent "if milestones are achieved in at least three out of the four reform areas.")

This "relaxation" will apply to only one year, 2020–21.[33]

Given that state governments' tax revenues have collapsed with the lockdowns, they have, inevitably, slashed their spending. For example, it is reported that the state government of Maharashtra has imposed a 67 percent cut on all developmental expenditure, a freeze on hiring, a halt to farm loan relief (already sanctioned), and a 25 percent cut in departmental expenses.[34] Similar cuts across all states would deepen the demand depression.

There could be no grimmer example of the consequences of this tight-fistedness than the field of public health—precisely the sector directly confronting COVID-19. The longstanding refusal of the government to spend on public health has laid the foundations for the present chaos and distress (see "Endnote: The Fiscal Starvation of Public Health").

This policy of fiscal starvation may have informed the government's choice of a lockdown as a "low-cost" strategy to tackle COVID-19. The extraordinary severity of India's lockdown no doubt won unstinted praise from international agencies (as being "comprehensive and robust" and "timely and tough").[35] But the simple truth is that, even ignoring any broader objections to such draconian measures, lockdowns do not in themselves reduce the ultimate number of deaths on account of the virus, no matter how "robust" or "tough" they be. In theory, they buy time to enable the authorities to expand and equip the health care system to cope with the flow of anticipated cases. A lockdown ought to be judged by its success or failure to achieve this task.[36]

However, for this to be the case, it would be essential to massively ramp up public health expenditure in order to hire a range of additional personnel, enhance the pay of existing low-paid personnel, set up more hospital beds, set up additional laboratories, buy additional equipment and materials, and so on. Since the lockdown also throws masses of people out of work and disrupts the supply of basic goods and services, rendering millions vulnerable to hunger, disease, and consequent death, it would equally be essential for the state to meet those basic needs, either directly or by providing people with cash with which to buy them. In both these respects, the central government's refusal to spend has had a devastating effect on the people.

So extreme has been the government's callousness that even the International Monetary Fund (IMF), the international high priest of fiscal austerity, signaled in April 2020 that the government could temporarily loosen its purse strings more than it had.[37] Thereafter, the government did come forward with a further stimulus package, but, as we saw, this too was among the world's most meagre. Why? We address this question in the following chapter.

ENDNOTE: THE FISCAL STARVATION OF PUBLIC HEALTH

There could be no grimmer example of the consequences of the government's tight-fistedness and how it serves private capital than the field of public health—precisely the sector that directly confronts COVID-19. The longstanding refusal of the government to spend on public health has laid the foundations for the present chaos and distress. Over the years, this policy has also fueled the growth of a large and profitable private sector in health care.

The relevant facts are summarized in a November 2019 report by the NITI Aayog, the Indian government's chief policymaking body. The report candidly acknowledges that the principal reason India's health system "lags behind comparable countries on multiple dimensions" is its low public expenditure:

India's fiscal funding of healthcare, around 1.0 per cent of GDP, is among the lowest in LMICs [low-middle income countries].... However, fiscal funding is likely to remain at 1.0–1.3 per cent of GDP. . . . The current one per cent of GDP as public financing for healthcare (and public health) will continue to constrain and limit the space for growth in the benefits package for the poor (although there is a commitment to increase this amount to 2.5 per cent of GDP as per the National Health Policy, 2017.[38]

While acknowledging that "there is an almost unanimous opinion among international health financing experts that financing a system through fiscal proceeds is the most efficient and equitable way to funding it," the report rules out this possibility: "waiting for such a substantial additional fiscal space as the only alternative, would mean that India would need to wait for decades until macroeconomic conditions allow for it."[39] Instead, the report promotes various types of health insurance.

It goes on to describe how the private sector expanded and flourished in the neoliberal era, finally accounting for 80 percent of outpatient and 60 percent of inpatient care:

Private healthcare providers have practiced in India since before Independence but constituted a small share of the provider market: only 8 per cent in 1947. Starting in the early 1980s, however, growth in private health enterprises started to pick up. The introduction of pro-market liberalization policies through-out the 1990s and 2000s, combined with under performance of public sector health services and weak regulatory mechanisms, has spurred exponential private sector growth.[40]

In 2010–11, there were an estimated 1.04 million private health enterprises across India, including roughly 80,000 private hospitals and 575,000 private medical clinics. The private sector thus employs 88 percent of doctors. By comparison, there were fewer than 200,000 government-run health care facilities across all provider levels in 2016.[41] They are understaffed: 69 percent of primary health centers function with only one or no doctor, and 65 percent of community health centers report a shortfall of specialists.[42]

Emptying People's Pockets

As a direct result of the government's refusal to spend, people are forced to divert their meagre incomes to health care. "Out of pocket expenditures" account for a staggering 64 percent of India's total

health expenditures, a higher percentage than in comparable economies. The sum India spends on health—about ₹5 trillion in 2015—is
not the problem; the problem is the breakup of these expenditures.
Thus, of India's total health expenses of nearly ₹5 trillion in 2015,
public expenditure accounted for only ₹1.1 trillion and contributory
schemes for ₹0.7 trillion. The burden of the remaining ₹3.2 trillion
was borne by out-of-pocket expenditures.[43]

The consequences for ordinary people are both financial and physical. The National Sample Survey found in 2017–18 that private sector
hospitalization costs were six times higher than the public sector ones
in rural areas, and eight times higher than the public sector costs in
urban areas. In the case of other medical treatments (that is, those not
involving hospitalization), the costs in the private sector were two to
three times those in the public sector.[44]

A recent study by an official thinktank calculates the impoverish-
ing effects of this policy.[45] It finds that, in 2014, about 23 percent of
Indian households faced "catastrophic payments" (defined as health
payments amounting to more than 10 percent of the total consumption expenditure of the household).[46] The share of households making
such catastrophic payments had increased over the decade between
2004 and 2014. Unsurprisingly, the poor are the main sufferers: the
headcount and intensity of catastrophic payments are higher among
poorer households.

Even using the official poverty lines (which are unconscionably
low), the study found that about *8–9 percent* of households, around
120 million people, were pushed below the poverty line in 2014 due
to health care payments—an appalling fact. Perhaps to avoid such a
fate, a fifth of the ill in both rural and urban areas deny themselves
treatment.[47]

Corporate Rise

The focus of government policy, however, is promoting the corporate
sector in health care, as the NITI Aayog acknowledges:

Large corporate chains and standalone hospitals dominate the top-end of the private market. Generally, these companies provide highly specialized services employing state-of-the-art technologies in tertiary and quaternary facilities located in major urban centres. Corporate chains have started to expand beyond major cities to establish large (100+ bed) hospitals in Tier II and III cities, indicating a desire to broaden their target demographic. This expansion has been encouraged by government, including through favourable tax policies.[48]

Oxfam acidly notes that "India manages to simultaneously rank 5th on the Medical Tourism Index and 145th among 195 countries [on the *Lancet* index] in terms of quality and accessibility of healthcare."[49]

Successive governments in India replaced the slogan "Health for All" with the subtly different "Universal Access to Health Care."[50] Instead of publicly financed, publicly provisioned health care, the major new health care initiatives by the central and state governments are subsidized health insurance schemes to fund access to care in private facilities—effectively subsidizing the private sector. "Most importantly, any increase in public expenditures would not build or strengthen the public health system but would further strengthen the private sector (especially the large tertiary care sector that increasingly is constituted by corporate run hospital chains)."[51]

Appalling Health Outcomes

This combination of a starved public sector and flourishing private sector is toxic for public health. Globally, an increase in public spending on health and public provision of health care leads to better and more efficiently achieved health outcomes, whereas an increase in private health care expenditure may actually be associated with higher mortality rates.[52] In India's case, government expenditure on health is less than one-fourth of total health expenditure. This contributes to India's considerably higher burden of disease and its lower global health care ranking, compared to similar economies.[53]

To take a single example, India has the dubious distinction of being the world leader in tuberculosis infections and deaths, with annual figures of nearly 3 million new cases and half a million deaths.[54] Tuberculosis in India is a disease essentially confined to the poor and malnourished population. Nevertheless, the fact that this curable disease is debilitating and killing such large numbers elicits no headlines or declarations of a national emergency.

Gates Foundation Influence

The process of growing corporate control has been crowned with the billionaire Bill Gates and his foundation acquiring extraordinary influence over India's public health policy. So great is Gates' authority that, in May 2020, Modi urged him to "take the lead in analysing the necessary changes in lifestyles, economic organisation, social behavior, modes of disseminating education, and healthcare, that would emerge in the post-COVID world." Gates' influence has been profoundly harmful: Whereas India needs to address the question of public health in a comprehensive way, encompassing nutrition, sanitation, drinking water, and preventive measures along with curative care, the Gates Foundation's public health model promotes the exact opposite: it puts private corporations in the driver's seat and assigns technological interventions the key role—a magic bullet for each disease. This will not ensure public health, but it will deliver private profits.

4

What Explains the Government's Refusal to Spend?

In this chapter, we look at two questions:

1. Why does the government fear increasing its expenditure, even in the face of an unprecedented crisis?
2. What is the government's alternative growth strategy, since it has ruled out any significant increase in spending?

Broadly speaking, the Indian government's refusal to spend is simply a more severe version of the policy followed by the world's weaker and dominated economies. As can be seen in Chart 1, there is a stark contrast between the restraint on the spending of the "low-income" countries and "emerging markets," on the one hand, and the advanced economies on the other (the G20 is a mixed grouping of advanced and "emerging" economies).

Specific Features of the Indian Government's Response

It is true that the Indian government's response has certain distinctive features, which bear the stamp of India's present rulers: sweeping

Chart 1: Fiscal Measures in Response to the COVID-19 Pandemic (percent of GDP)

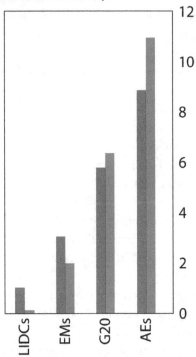

Additional spending and foregone revenue
Loans, equity and guarantees

LIDCs = low-income developing countries; EMs = emerging markets; G20 = group of twenty; AEs = advanced economies. Source: IMF Fiscal Affairs Department, "Fiscal Monitor Database of Country Fiscal Measures in Response to the COVID-19 Pandemic," International Monetary Fund, June 2020.

autocratic edicts, indifference to mass misery, monumental mismanagement, and widespread coercion. These features have greatly intensified, even multiplied, the misery and despair experienced by millions. It is necessary to sketch them, however briefly, before returning to our main theme.

According to a recent report, the government delayed action on early warnings from its own top medical advisors to begin preparation for a coming COVID-19 pandemic.[55] It imposed a sudden, sweeping virtual curfew on a nation of 1.3 billion with four hours of notice. It did this despite specific advice in February 2020 from its advisors to refrain from a sweeping lockdown and to instead opt for "community and civil society-led self-quarantine and self-monitoring."[56] The first announcement of lockdown was for twenty-one days, on the stated grounds that this period was "extremely critical to break the infection chain of coronavirus," but before it expired, the lockdown was extended to fifty-four days and then to sixty-eight days.[57]

Two weeks into the lockdown, the government's scientist advisors reportedly complained that this period was not being used effectively to set up the necessary public health teams and infrastructure to tackle the inevitable surge of cases when the lockdown was lifted.[58] There were widespread complaints of the absence of protective gear or testing kits for frontline workers; the government appears to have placed orders extremely late.[59] In fact, it has now become evident that the lockdown was a fiasco, in effect achieving nothing but the economic and physical exhaustion of the country, leaving the people as exposed to the virus and as bereft of health infrastructure as before, but now even poorer.[60]

Millions of migrant workers—men, women, and children—were stranded without livelihoods or food. When they set out, many of them on foot, for their villages, they faced severe police retaliation, with the Home Ministry issuing orders to restrict movement and the Haryana police ordering fleeing workers to be jailed in stadiums and other facilities.[61] The press reported an appalling paucity of relief for desperate workers and their families stranded, either in the cities or along the way. In rural areas, agricultural marketing and supply chains were disrupted due to lack of planning.[62]

Surveys of the impact of the lockdown carried out by a wide range of organizations and institutions clearly show that "livelihoods have been devastated at unprecedented levels. Food insecurity and economic vulnerability have increased to staggering proportions. Hunger deaths and suicides linked to economic stress are being reported from various parts of the country."[63] Indian women, already victims of an outsized gender gap in employment, wages, and education, suffered the steepest economic loss of the lockdown, as well as a harsh rise in domestic violence and drudgery.[64]

The manner in which the government imposed and enforced the lockdown contradicted even its stated purpose—namely, public health. It drastically affected incomes and nutrition, in turn affecting health, and disrupted routine medical services and vaccinations. Three instances are worth pointing to: (1) The lockdown-related reduction in nutrition is estimated to have led to an additional 186,000 tuberculosis cases and 86,000 deaths.[65] (2) Given the large number of children in India clustered around the undernutrition threshold, the lockdown is estimated to have caused a stark increase in the prevalence of child underweight and wasting among the poorest children in India.[66] (3) COVID-19-related disruptions to the country's immunization and vaccination programs have created a real risk of a measles outbreak.[67]

The focus of the state machinery was instead on enforcing the lockdown with armed force, treating infringements as criminal acts. Thus, the deaths of a father and son in Tamil Nadu under heinous police torture, for the crime of having kept their shop open longer than permitted, was a natural outcome of this policy. The chief minister of another state, Telangana, actually threatened to issue shoot-on-sight orders to enforce the lockdown, all ludicrously in the name of public health.

All these actions and measures reflect the reality of the Indian political system, which possesses the paraphernalia of democracy but functions as an autocracy. Its present stewards have added a greater level of coercion and a more fascistic hue to the system. Domination of mass and social media, as well as considerable skill in exploiting religious symbols and communal and caste divisions, help obscure the system's responsibility for these manmade calamities.

Clear Divisions

However, the extraordinary tight-fistedness of the government's policy is not on account of India's rulers' specific traits. Rather, it flows from the position of India's economy within the world economy and the government's anxiety to woo foreign financial investors, who are opposed in general to increased government spending by third world countries. This reality is bluntly stated by the most authoritative sources, as we show.

Before proceeding, we need to remember that global finance makes a clear division: there are a handful of powerful countries that dominate the world economy and there are weaker economies, like India's, which account for the bulk of the world's population. (The latter are no doubt rich sources of cheap sweated labor and precious resources, but that wealth has been devalued and continues to be further devalued through a long historical process.) In the world of global finance, no one pays attention to the breathless claims that India is a rising power and will imminently be considered a developed country. They simply see it as a poor and weak country, a source of rich pickings in good times, but one that can be dumped in the bad.

The currencies of powerful countries, "hard currencies" or "reserve currencies", are accepted as payment between countries, meaning that they operate as world money. The leading currency is still the U.S. dollar. The United States can thus unilaterally expand the supply of dollars and make payments to others in its own currency, but other countries cannot do the same. In particular, the spending of weak economies is restricted even in the direst calamities, as evidenced by chart 1.

India's rulers have long adopted a development path that hitches India's economy to inflows of foreign capital, a trend that has deepened over the years. While India in 2019 owned foreign assets worth 25 percent of its GDP, its foreign liabilities were much larger, at 40 percent of GDP. Thus, its *net foreign liabilities* were 15 percent of GDP, or $455 billion, in 2019.[68] Capital that has flowed in can also flow out, particularly in the case of purely financial investments (in the stock market and the debt market), which are not tied down in physical assets here. If foreign financial investors were to decide to rapidly withdraw their investments, the stock market would crash (as it has done periodically in the past with even partial withdrawals) and the rupee's exchange rate would plummet.

As a result, it is foreign investors who hold the whip in hand and can shape the policies of the Indian government. Foreign investors' interests are ably represented by credit ratings agencies—Moody's, Standard and Poor, and Fitch Ratings. These agencies rate the ability of an entity to service its debts and the chances it will default. They assign borrowers grades, not unlike the grades given to children in school, such as AAA, BBB+, and so on. Not only are companies rated like this, but so are sovereign countries. Their access to overseas credit and the interest rates at which they borrow depend on the ratings assigned by these three agencies. Indeed, if a country is "downgraded," not only will it find it harder to borrow, but foreign investors may withdraw their investments from the country to one extent or the other.

A "speculative" rating—or, in common parlance, a "junk" rating—means that there is a high chance of the borrower defaulting and, accordingly, the interest rate is higher on these borrowings. Moreover, foreign investors look more favorably on a country with a better rating. Fitch and Standard & Poor both rate India one grade above a junk rating. Moody's had rated it two grades above junk, but on June 1, 2020, reduced it to one grade above junk, citing India's increasing fiscal stress.

Clear Warnings

The present chief economic advisor to the government has warned that countries with a credit rating similar to India's have given small stimulus packages and India would have to do so as well.[69] Indeed, Fitch Ratings has already raised the alarm regarding India's fiscal deficit in the wake of COVID-19: "The country has limited fiscal space to respond to the challenges posed by the health crisis.... Further deterioration in the fiscal outlook as a result of lower growth or fiscal easing could pressure the sovereign rating in light of the limited fiscal headroom India had when it entered this crisis."[70]

Government officials involved in preparing the government's COVID-19 economic package told *Reuters* quite bluntly: 'We have to be cautious as downgrades have started happening for some countries and *rating agencies treat developed nations and emerging markets very differently*. . . . We have already done 0.8% of GDP, we might have space for another 1.5%–2% GDP."[71] In fact, the government's announcements in May fell short of even this figure.

The last three governors of India's central bank weighed in with their views. All three explicitly drew the line between the developed world and countries like India. In London's *Financial Times*, ex-governor D. Subbarao sternly warned that India must restrict itself to a fixed amount of additional borrowing and plan to reverse the action once the crisis blows over:

> Global markets are much less forgiving of unconventional policies by emerging market central banks. . . . Rich countries can afford to throw the kitchen sink at the crisis [i.e., do whatever it takes] because they have the firepower and they issue debt in currencies that others crave…emerging markets don't have that luxury.[72]

Ex-governor Urjit Patel similarly cautioned that

> hardly any emerging market economy (EME), with the possible exception of China, can match, what developed countries like the US, UK and Germany, for instance, have announced. These countries have basically set out, at least in the short run, to offset, through generous direct government entitlements to large sections of the population and extraordinary central bank activism, the adverse demand shock following the primary negative supply shock of the pandemic. Countries that can issue reserve currencies have much more elbow room. *EMEs, like India, obviously don't have this luxury.*[73]

What would happen if India tried to imitate the developed countries and took substantial measures to cushion its population from shock? Foreign investors, he warned, would get "spooked":

If the fiscal and monetary responses are overdone, the likelihood of non-trivial consequences for macroeconomic stability increases. . . . Foreign portfolio investment in Indian equity and bonds is about US$ 300 billion. US$ 15 billion exited last month, and that is not a surprise. . . . Our macroeconomic management should not be the driver to spook investors.

In a crisis, he pointed out, "there is a flight to safety, essentially investment in US government bonds, with home country bias also coming into play when global risks flare up. The exorbitant privilege of the US dollar not only endures, it is reinforced during crisis."[74]

While ex-governor Raghuram Rajan spared a few more words for "spending on the needy," he too was blunt about the limits:

Unlike the United States or Europe, which can spend 10% more of GDP without fear of a ratings downgrade, we already entered this crisis with a huge fiscal deficit, and will have to spend yet more. . . .

A ratings downgrade coupled with a loss of investor confidence could lead to a plummeting exchange rate and a dramatic increase in long term interest rates in this environment, and substantial losses for our financial institutions.

Rajan proposed guaranteeing foreign investors that any immediate increase in spending would be followed by a reduction in spending, enforced by an "independent fiscal council."[75] In other words, he suggested that future fiscal control be taken out of the hands of the government and put in the hands of an "independent" body effectively taking its cues from foreign investors.[76]

Note that these former governors and India's chief economic advisor did not estimate the permissible size of a stimulus package on the basis of the projected loss of GDP and thus project the need for government spending in that light. They simply, and quite frankly, said that only such-and-such amount would be *allowed* by the credit rating agencies. In this way, they made it quite explicit that *the frame of domestic economic policy is not determined domestically, but abroad, without any involvement by the Indian people.*

Rickety Foundations

The three governors cannot be faulted for saying that foreign investors may punish India for expanding its government spending by withdrawing their capital and that a crisis would ensue, given the present nature of the Indian economy. We may differ with the prescription that flows from their analysis, but not with their contention that India's economic foundations are rickety.

Foreign investors withdrew $83 billion from what are termed "emerging" markets globally at the start of the crisis, the largest capital outflow ever recorded.[77] They withdrew $16 billion from India's "emerging" equity and debt markets in March alone—the highest ever for a single month and the highest for any country that month.[78]

At first glance, it seems that India should have nothing to fear from a flight of foreign investors, since it has huge foreign exchange reserves: $534.6 billion as of July 31, 2020. However, these reserves are not as impressive as they look, since they have been built not through current account surpluses (that is, not by earning more foreign exchange than we spend), but by increasing the sum we *owe* foreigners—foreign debt and foreign investments. These liabilities impose a drain on the country in "normal" times, but at times of crisis do not necessarily protect the country from ruin. Yet, in the existing frame of India's economy, there is a compulsion to keep accumulating more and more reserves, with more and more corresponding liabilities. (One study indeed termed the foreign exchange reserves not a "shield of comfort," but an "albatross" around the neck of India.[79]) As we describe in the endnote "India's Foreign Exchange Reserves—How Much Protection Do They Offer from a Sudden Exit of Foreign Capital?," India's foreign exchange reserves can be rapidly depleted in case of a grave crisis. Of course, India is not yet facing a crisis of this nature on the foreign exchange front, and such crises are rare. But when they occur, they can have devastating consequences.

The Growth Model: Relying on Aggressive "Reforms" and Privatization to Arouse the Accumulation Drive of Private Investors

As we have seen above, the reason for the government's refusal to spend is that it is keenly sensitive to the demands and ultimatums of foreign investors, and thus tailors domestic economic policy accordingly. (There is an alternative to this policy, as we shall see, but this alternative lies outside the present setup.)

The components of GDP (measured from the demand side) are consumer spending, government spending, business investment, and net exports. We know that consumers' incomes have fallen steeply, exports will not grow amid a global recession, and the government is restraining its own expenditure. As these sources of demand remain depressed, businesses—already saddled with excess capacity—are unlikely to invest in creating fresh capacity.

Where, then, will growth come from? Evidently, the government's plans for stimulating growth are focused on arousing the so-called *animal spirits* (or, more appropriately, *predator spirits*) of private capital by carrying out what are nowadays called "reforms."[80] That is, the government promises the corporate sector higher returns by reducing wages, subsidizing land, and subsidizing loans. This was the real content of the prime minister's speech to the nation on May 12, when he announced a new package of measures: "In order to prove the resolve of a self-reliant India, Land, Labor, Liquidity and Laws all have been emphasized in this package."[81]

Of course, the costs of spurring the accumulation drive of private capital are to be borne by workers, who will be more severely exploited and even physically endangered; peasants, whose lands will be forcibly acquired; and all working people, as capital, including bank credit, is to be even further concentrated in the corporate sector.

The chief economic advisor spelled out the growth model:

"Land and labour are really factor market reforms because these are factor inputs that really affect the cost of doing business and you have seen a lot of changes on these recently at state level."

Uttar Pradesh, Madhya Pradesh and Gujarat have announced fundamental labour reforms and other states are also in line to follow up, he said, adding, Karnataka had just gone ahead and changed the regulation on acquisition of land for business.

Land can now be directly bought from farmers in the state and other states will also imbibe the model.[82]

The old land reform law in Karnataka prevented direct acquisition of land by private business in order to protect peasants from force and fraud. The scrapping of this protection has been immediately welcomed by big business but protested vigorously by peasant organizations.[83]

Finance minister Nirmala Sitharaman presented the economic package in press conferences over the course of five days. By the third day, it was evident that the promise of a ₹20 trillion package was a sleight of hand. Indeed, the last installment contained no mention of government expenditure; it did not even pretend to stimulate demand. It was composed solely of the unbridled privatization of everything—coal, minerals, defense production (where "self-reliance" is to be achieved by raising the limit of foreign investment from 49 percent to 74 percent), civil aviation, power distribution, atomic energy, and space.

Similarly, the finance minister's announcement of agricultural "reforms" was not addressed to the peasantry, but to the corporate sector, to enable it to penetrate agriculture more freely. There was not a word about government procurement of various types of agricultural produce at remunerative prices, which is what the peasantry has been demanding (at present, such government procurement is restricted largely to rice and wheat and is carried out only in a few states). Instead, the finance minister presented a plan for capitalists—processors, aggregators, large retailers, exporters—to procure directly from the peasants. A key part of the plan is to remove all controls on private trade in agricultural products. On September 20, 2020, the government forced three legislations through parliament, giving effect to its plans for agriculture.

Ever since the finance minister's announcement, peasant organizations have been staging protests against this package "for agriculture." These protests turned into a significant upsurge in September 2020. They understand clearly that this is a step toward ending all government procurement of crops from the peasantry, including rice and wheat, dealing peasant farming a lethal blow. It will leave them entirely in the grip of private trade, including corporate firms.

The rulers' growth model, then, relies nearly exclusively on private investors to revive growth. Accordingly, the message that India's rulers wish to send out to foreign investors and large domestic capital is that *COVID-19 has freed them from all earlier social restraints.* More than the details of different sectors' "reform" measures, what is significant is their extraordinary sweep, their utter arbitrariness, and their unilateral, summary disposal of rights that had been won by the people of the world and of India through struggle and sacrifice.

Open Season on Laborers

Speaking to chief ministers of state governments on April 27, the prime minister urged them to follow the example of the state of Rajasthan, which had permitted a twelve-hour working day with the excuse that COVID-19 had made labor scarce. Modi candidly termed the present crisis an "opportunity." "We have to carry out reforms too," he said. "If a state takes an initiative for reform, we can *turn this crisis into a big opportunity.*"

What exactly was the "opportunity" to which he referred? Perhaps it was opportunity to push through changes at a time when, due to the lockdown, workers' organizations were unable to mobilize mass protests and the atmosphere of the current all-enveloping health and economic crisis provided the authorities liberal cover. Seizing this opportunity, nine state governments—Uttar Pradesh, Madhya Pradesh, Gujarat, Rajasthan, Haryana, Uttarakhand, Himachal Pradesh, Assam, and Goa—announced the suspension of various labor laws and parts of laws.

It would be difficult to imagine a more candid declaration of class affiliation. The Uttar Pradesh government's ordinance, for example, simply exempts all factories and establishments engaged in manufacturing processes from *all labor laws* for a period of three years, albeit with certain conditions. Most of the state governments specifically allowed the working day to be extended to eleven or twelve hours—a stunning throwback to the nineteenth century.

These measures are useless for the purpose of stimulating fresh industrial investment. All capitalists would prefer to pay lower wages to their own workers and thus increase their individual profits, but the investment decisions of private investors, domestic and foreign, do not depend mainly on labor costs. In a situation of acutely depressed demand, capitalists are not interested in creating new capacity. Large capitalists' expenditure in this period tends to be focused on taking over existing assets, and indeed this is what has been taking place in India.

What will be the impact of the suspension of labor laws in various states? These laws apply to only a tiny fraction of India's workforce. Over 75 percent of the workforce are self-employed or casual laborers (including in agriculture), while the remainder are regular wage workers. Less than 10 percent of the workforce are regular wage workers receiving even one social security benefit; just 4 percent of the workforce receive comprehensive social security cover—that is, Provident Fund/pension, gratuity, health care, and maternity benefits—and just 2 percent have comprehensive cover and written contracts for three years or more.[84]

The fact that labor laws cover a small percentage of workers is cited in diametrically opposite ways by employers and working-class organizations. Employers profess tender sympathy for the workers not covered by the laws, claim that a tiny minority of protected workers are preventing the vast majority from getting better jobs, and press for the scrapping of these laws. Working-class organizations, on the other hand, point out that these laws, which codify the bare minimum of subsistence, safe working conditions, job security, and the right to organize, represent an immediate practical aim of struggle for the whole working class. If the very laws are demolished, and even the limited sections of the working class that possess these minimal rights are pushed down, the entire class will suffer.

The real significance of the so-called labor reforms is thus not limited to the specific provisions of the various acts that stand suspended. Rather, the aim is to demolish the very *idea* that laborers should have rights, that they can engage in disputes with their employers, and that there can be social restraints on bosses. It is to inculcate this thinking in the workers themselves and set them in brutal competition with one another instead of uniting as a class.

For the moment, suspensions of labor laws by state governments face legal challenges in the courts. Meanwhile, on September 23, 2020, the Indian government foisted a more permanent change, replacing twenty-five national-level labor laws with three new "labor codes." These new codes (1) make it easier for employers to fire workers or unilaterally change their employment conditions; (2) enable firms to use "fixed-term" employees instead of workers with job security; (3) prevent "outsiders" from becoming office-bearers of trade unions, thereby obstructing unionization; (4) make it much more difficult to strike legally; and (5) penalize workers who join "illegal" strikes. Overnight, Indian workers' few legal protections have been drastically abridged.

The editor of *Business Standard* unabashedly welcomes the manner in which COVID-19 is undoing labor rights in practice:

> This protected world of assured jobs, wages, and pensions (spelling a modest if secure existence) related to just a sixth of the workforce. The rest were in the informal sector, where it was a free-for-all and you were lucky to even get a proper letter of employment. While the term "labour aristocracy" overstates the case, there were signs that the dichotomy was becoming intolerable; Covid-19 has simply hastened the denouement.… If Covid-19 helps restore some rationality in these and other areas, its legacy may not be entirely destructive.[85]

Demolition of Environmental Laws

The COVID-19 crisis offers a similarly "big opportunity" for the demolition of environmental legislation and for the corporate takeover of natural resources.

As in the case of labor laws, the legal protections for the environment have been largely, even overwhelmingly, breached in practice. India's Environmental Impact Assessments, introduced in 1994, are meant to assess the entire range of likely ecological impacts of various types of projects and provide a basis for their obtaining or being denied clearances. Environmentalists have long argued that these are purely formal and serve merely as a legitimizing tool, as "the rejection rate under EIA [Environmental Impact Assessments] is nearly zero."[86] Nevertheless, the rulers were so far unable to entirely eliminate the scope for contestation of environmental clearances, including through provisions in the law for public consultation and public hearings in which the affected people could voice their views. Such provisions could on occasion be used by the struggling local people and democratically minded citizens in the course of specific agitations against destructive projects and land acquisitions.

The latest draft notification of India's environment ministry—issued at the start of the nationwide lockdown—aims to eliminate any such possibility. All so-called linear projects, such as roads or pipelines, no longer require environmental clearance. The projects of some forty industries no longer require public consultation. These include projects with very serious environmental impacts, such as irrigation projects (with a command area of two thousand to ten thousand hectares); coal and non-coal mineral prospecting; solar photovoltaic projects; offshore and onshore exploration for oil, gas, and shale; expansion of highways between twenty-five and one hundred kilometers; construction projects up to 150,000 square meters; and so on. Any project the government considers "strategic" is exempted, as are all national highways and inland waterways. Project expansions up to 25 percent will not require an environmental impact assessment and up to 50 percent will not require public consultation.

Several other provisions make clear that the purpose of the notification is to do away with the very idea that there should be social control over the actions of private capitalists. For example, the draft innovates a unique legislative scheme for law breaking: it allows *post facto* clearances (better termed *fait accompli* clearances). That is, a firm can start a project without clearances, carry out environmental destruction, and apply for clearance later.

Even more audacious is the provision that *excludes the public from reporting violations and non-compliance.* The government will take cognizance only of reports by government bodies or the *project proponent* (the violator).

The Modi government has stepped up pressure to amend or water down existing environmental laws and, if necessary, replace them. A new Draft National Forest Policy and a Draft Coastal Regulation Zone notification appeared in 2018. The government has been clearing projects at breakneck speed. An *IndiaSpend* analysis suggests that the Modi government has issued clearances at the rate of more than one a day since 2014, including 278 projects in and immediately around the most ecologically sensitive locations.[87] Under the Modi government, the diversion of nearly fifteen thousand square kilometers of forest land has received approval or is awaiting approval, a sharp increase over the earlier period.[88]

Seizing the opportunity provided by the COVID-19 lockdown, India's environment ministry has been issuing environment, forest, and wildlife clearances through two-hour video conferences of expert panels, dispensing with actual meetings. Experts admitted to the press that the time allotted for considering some of the projects is very little, in some cases just ten minutes per project. Due to the lockdown, neither can affected people send evidence or representations, nor can expert panelists conduct field visits. It was reported that 191 projects were to be considered in this fashion in April and May 2020.[89]

A particularly alarming decision is the auction of forty new coalfields in some of India's most ecologically sensitive forests, including the Hasdeo Arand forest in Chhattisgarh. This and several other areas now slated for mining had been designated under the previous government as "no-go" areas due to their rich biodiversity. At the time, the environment ministry was criticized for too narrow a definition. However, even these "no-go" areas have been reduced by more than 80 percent under the present government. Resistance by the local people faces unfavorable odds: among the main beneficiaries of the mining project is the corporate chieftain Gautam Adani, well-known for his long-standing closeness to Modi.[90]

When the Modi government initially tried to amend the Land Acquisition, Rehabilitation, and Resettlement Act of 2013 to the disadvantage of the peasantry, it faced widespread opposition and decided to drop the amendment for the moment. Land acquisition is one of the important flashpoints of class struggle in the country today: Land Conflict Watch India has documented 703 sites of conflict over land acquisition, spread over 2.1 million hectares of land, and affecting 6.5 million people.[91] However, land is also one of the four promises ("Land, Labor, Liquidity and Laws") the prime minister made to private investors in his May 12 "self-reliance" speech. We may now expect a fresh effort to separate peasants from their lands in order to offer it to the corporate sector.

The blanket destruction of labor's legal rights and environmental protections bears a resemblance to various actions of the present regime and its political cadres in other spheres. These actions are aimed at wiping out the very sources of rights and inculcating a change in the psyche of the people. If the physical existence of a mosque represents a claim by Muslims to be treated as equal citizens, the mosque must be destroyed and replaced by a grand temple. If the meagre remaining protections under Articles 35 and 370 of the Indian Constitution, however diluted, remind one of the specific historical circumstances of Kashmir's joining to India and the basis for Kashmiris' demand for freedom, these constitutional provisions themselves must be scrapped; the very constitutional unit of Jammu and Kashmir must be eliminated permanently and replaced by two principalities of the central government. If history textbooks contain facts and perspectives that inculcate secular values, the textbooks themselves must be scrapped and replaced, indeed a new education policy must be imposed. If certain universities continue to teach students to think for themselves, these universities must themselves be, for all practical purposes, demolished and replaced with teaching shops staffed by followers of the regime. To symbolically mark this remaking of Indian society, the public architecture of the country's capital must itself be radically remodeled. These various measures are framed by the proclamation that this is a "New India," a statement intended to overawe and demoralize those who may resist. COVID-19 has provided a further opportunity for such attacks. Significantly, across the board, the government has persisted on its course even at the height of the COVID-19 crisis.

What the Rulers Mean by "Self-Reliance"

The prime minister's May 12 speech, in which he introduced the theme of *Atmanirbharta*, or "self-reliance," excited some anxious commentary from liberal pundits who felt that the government was about to reverse three decades of neoliberal reform. They failed to read the speech itself, which made clear that this vision of "self-reliance" aims at integrating India more closely into global supply chains:

Self-reliance also prepares the country for a tough competition in the global supply chain. And today it is the need of the hour that India should play a big role in the global supply chain. Realizing this, many provisions have also been made in the economic package. This will increase the efficiency of all our sectors and also ensure quality.

Eager to dispel the notion that, by "self-reliance," he actually meant self-reliance, Modi followed this up by addressing foreign investors at the India Global Week 2020 virtual conference.

India remains one of the most open economies of the world. We are laying a red carpet for all global companies to come and establish their presence in India. Very few countries will offer the kind of opportunity that India does today," Modi said. . . .

Modi said there are possibilities and opportunities in various sunrise sectors in India. "Our reforms in agriculture provide a very active investment opportunity to invest in storage and logistics. We are opening the doors to the investors to come and invest directly in the hard work of our farmers. . . .

With relaxed FDI [foreign direct investment] norms, one of the world's biggest militaries invites you to come and make products for it. . . .

Modi said 130 crore [1.3 billion] Indians have given a call for self-reliance. *A self-reliant India merges domestic production and consumption with global supply chains.* "AtmaNirbhar Bharat [a self-reliant India] is not about self-contained or being closed to the world.[92]

The current public health crisis, too, offers a business opportunity of sorts. Addressing the United States-India Business Council on July 22, the prime minister pointed out that the health care sector in India is growing faster than 22 percent every year. "*Now is the best time,*" he urged, "*to expand your investment in the Indian healthcare sector.*"[93]

The Unanswered Question

We have discussed the reasons for the rulers' refusal to spend and how they propose to revive "growth" in the absence of demand. The framework, as we saw, is set by foreign investors' opposition to government spending. But the question remains: Why do foreign investors oppose government spending?

On this question, the RBI governors and the present and past chief economic advisors are silent. Sometimes silence is more revealing than what is said. We turn to this question in the next chapter.

Endnote: India's Foreign Exchange Reserves—How Much Protection Do They Offer from a Sudden Exit of Foreign Capital?

On the face of it, India's foreign exchange reserves appear comfortable. Indeed, since the start of 2020, the reserves have actually risen nearly a whopping $75 billion (as of July 31, 2020). At present, they are well over the value of a normal year's imports. So, is India not fully protected against a possible foreign exchange crisis?

In the past, foreign exchange crises in developing countries used to be triggered by a sudden rise in their import costs (as when oil-importing countries faced a sudden oil price hike) or a collapse in their export revenues. However, as international financial flows have expanded massively in the era of globalization, the current danger for foreign exchange reserves comes not from import requirements, but from capital movements—a rapid withdrawal of foreign investments and deposits, and a sudden stop to fresh capital inflows. A number of third world countries—Mexico (1995), several East Asian countries (1997), Brazil (1999), Turkey (1994, 2001, 2018), Argentina (2002, 2018–present) bear testimony to this.

Particularly in the wake of the 1997 East Asian crisis, developing countries have felt compelled to insure themselves against such episodes, increasing their foreign exchange reserves tenfold (from $646 billion in 2000 to $6.3 trillion in 2015). However, given the steady growth of capital flows and the buildup of external liabilities, it is difficult to predict how much would be adequate. Moreover, the question is not only how much is required to take care of a crisis, but how much is required to reassure foreign investors and creditors of the creditworthiness of the country, thereby protecting the country from a "loss of confidence."[94]

In India's case, it is important to keep in mind that its foreign exchange reserves are not built out of trade surpluses. In fact, India consistently runs trade and current account deficits, that is, it needs to borrow simply in order to meet its current payments. When inflows exceed India's current financing needs, they add to the reserves. Thus, India's reserves are made up of foreign capital inflows, which correspondingly increase India's liabilities to foreigners.

Let us look at a few facts. The latest detailed data we have are for the end of 2019.

1. At the end of December 2019, India's foreign exchange reserves were $459.9 billion. However, at $563.9 billion, India's external debt was more than $100 billion larger than its reserves.

2. The RBI calculates a figure called "short term external debt by *residual maturity*." This refers to external debts due within twelve months (including long-term debts that fall due within a year). This figure comes to $238.3 billion at the end of December 2019.

   Apart from debt, India also has other external liabilities—foreign investment, both direct investment (FDI) and foreign portfolio investment (FPI), in particular. While FDI is meant to be longer term and cannot be repatriated quickly, FPI can be withdrawn instantly. The RBI reports that by the end of December 2019, FPIs had amounted to $148.9 billion in shares and $117.8 billion in debt instruments. Even though this way of reporting greatly understates the liability, total FPI comes to $266.7 billion.[95]

   Adding the above two figures—short term debt by residual maturity ($238.3 billion) and liabilities to FPIs ($266.7 billion)— we get a sum of $505 billion at the end of December 2019, that is, $45.1 billion *more* than the foreign exchange reserves on that date. This indicates that, if fresh foreign loans and investment are not forthcoming, the seemingly large foreign exchange reserves can fall steeply over the course of the coming year.

3. More relevant, however, is the sum that can be withdrawn very rapidly from the country. It is this that presents a more concrete danger. This applies to two types of non-resident Indian deposits: Non-Resident (External) Rupee Accounts and Foreign Currency Non-Resident (Bank) Accounts, totaling $116.9 billion, and FPI

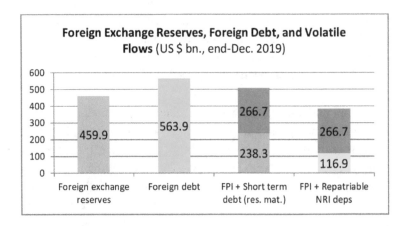

investment, at $266.7 billion. The sum comes to $383.6 billion. That means this foreign investors and depositors could, at a moment's notice, withdraw a sum amounting to more than 83 percent of the foreign reserves.

In India's own case, during the 1990–91 foreign exchange crisis, non-resident Indian deposits were withdrawn very rapidly from the country. It is true that this does not seem likely to happen now, since it has not happened for nearly three decades.[96] India has suffered three recent episodes—in 2013, 2018, and March-April 2020—of sizable capital exits, along with sharp rupee depreciation.

Moreover, the world economy is now in uncharted waters and it is risky to assume that earlier patterns will hold. A sudden stop in capital flows has had a dramatic impact even on economies that appeared stronger and stabler than India is today (such as South Korea in 1997). And strangely, an external crisis in one third world country can trigger a sudden stop in flows to other third world countries, by "contagion" as foreign investors "lose confidence," irrespective of the specificities of the other countries.

As for the share market, it is true that, as foreign investors sell shares, share prices would fall, as would the rupee's value, thus reducing what those investors would get in hand. There would therefore seem to be a sort of self-correcting mechanism preventing a flight of FPI investments. But we know from experience worldwide that, in a situation of crisis, foreign investors might fear losing all, move as a herd, and accept drastically reduced prices in order to cut their losses.[97]

In sum, under extraordinary circumstances, the foreign exchange reserves are not protected from rapid drawdown. Periodic panics serve as reminders of this fact and extract their price in the form of emergency measures taken by the government to calm foreign investors. Even if a dramatic collapse never actually occurs, the *possibility* conditions the government's responses and ensures that it toes the line drawn by the credit rating agencies and the IMF. Systematic obedience, then, is the real significance of the picture we have sketched.

Of course, the rulers will not contemplate an alternative course, freeing the country of dependence on foreign capital, as that would go against the class forces they represent.

In the last few months, we have seen a sudden return of foreign investment in India's share markets. The flood of dollars has led to the share markets surging, the rupee's value recovering, and the foreign exchange reserves swelling. However, this is not driven by any improvement in the Indian economy's prospects or the strengthening of its foundations—quite the contrary is evident from the data available. The inflow of dollars is due simply to the extraordinary measures being taken by the U.S. Federal Reserve and the U.S. government, which have pumped out vast quantities of dollars and reduced interest rates to near zero. Correspondingly, this means that there is nothing secure or stable about these inflows: they are speculative funds, which may exit at any time based on changes in U.S. interest rates, the bursting of the bubble in U.S. markets, and so on.

5

Why Do Foreign Investors Oppose Government Spending in India?

Summary

The standard explanations given for foreign investors' opposition to government spending in India—namely, that foreign investors are worried about inflation, or that they are worried there will be runaway growth of government debt—are unconvincing. An additional explanation, that foreign investors oppose government spending because of their neoliberal "ideology," is inadequate: the same foreign investors embrace government spending in their home countries whenever it suits their own interests, such as when the government there bails out the financial sector during each crisis.

The real reason for foreign investors' systematic opposition to government spending in countries like India is that, when such spending is suppressed, private investment is the only game in town. In such a situation, private investors are able to extract various concessions from the government as the cost of being persuaded to invest. Furthermore, during a regime of fiscal cuts, the government carries out so-called reforms in favor of big capitalists and sells off valuable public assets at distress prices in the name of bridging the fiscal deficit. These are major windfall gains for private capitalists and, in crisis periods, foreign capitalists are best positioned to take advantage of these opportunities. In turn, the lack of government spending aggravates the paucity of demand in the economy and pushes a large number of domestic private firms to sell off their assets at depressed prices. Foreign investors, relatively flush with funds from the economic stimulus packages in their home countries, are then able to step in and buy prize assets very cheaply. The crises suffered by South Korea, Thailand, and Greece are striking illustrations of this process.

In India, there is an endemic paucity of demand due to the stultifying basic features of India's political economy, and these will not change in the existing setup. Given this constraint, episodes of rapid growth take place only when there is some special stimulus, and they peter out rapidly. India's rapid growth of 2003–08 was actually a credit boom, or bubble, produced by large inflows of foreign finance. The boom, and the prospects of rapid accumulation of wealth, also whetted the appetite of large Indian capitalists to grab public assets, subsidies, and natural resources. One way of doing this was through public-private partnerships, which were funded by public sector banks. Fraud and diversion of funds by private investors were rampant.

With the Global Financial Crisis, there was a sudden stop to capital inflows, a credit freeze, and general uncertainty, and of course growth slowed. Initially, the government had a clear go-ahead from the leading capitalist countries to revive growth by expanding spending, which enabled it to recover by 2009–10. However, once global finance found its feet again, it applied pressure for fiscal cutbacks in third world countries like India.

Given India's underlying problem of demand and the deflation of the bubble growth of 2003–08, the only means of stimulating growth that remained was government spending and, to a lesser extent, the easing of credit (by reducing interest rates and other measures). However, both weapons were slowly surrendered in the post-2010 period. The central government brought down its spending to GDP ratio sharply. The country's central bank, the RBI, adopted a one-point objective of bringing down inflation and went about doing so by, in effect, deflating the incomes of working people.

During the earlier period, between 2003 and 2010, bank credit to the private corporate sector swelled massively as large capitalists expanded at breakneck speed. Once the bubble burst, the corporate borrowers began defaulting on their loans, which became non-performing assets. The private corporate sector turned to massive external commercial borrowings, ignoring the risks. (Meanwhile, small and medium firms were starved of credit and faced repeated blows from government policies, causing them to begin shrinking.)

The growing contradiction between foreign liabilities and a weakening economic base must at some point end in either of two resolutions: the *repudiation* of the foreign liabilities (which is not in the cards in the existing social order) or the *transfer* of domestic assets to foreign capital. The RBI's tightening of norms for recognizing bad debt and the introduction of the Insolvency and Bankruptcy Code were important steps on the second course.

Thus, as a result of the private corporate sector's debt spree, followed by a long period of stagnation/decline in productive activity, **a major restructuring of the Indian economy is in the works.** Labor is being restructured in favor of capital: small firms are being restructured or destroyed in favor of big capital, the public sector is being cannibalized by private capital, and the domestic economy as a whole is being restructured in favor of foreign capital.

This process is already under way. Assets of the private corporate sector are being taken over by foreign investors on a sizable scale and the present sharp downturn of the economy is likely to speed up this process. This takeover will carry with it all the negative features of the initial projects but will also have the added negative traits of foreign ownership.

The privatization program itself is an even more audacious annexation of national assets by foreign capital as well as by large Indian firms. The manner in which the government is attempting to sell off one of its most precious assets, the highly profitable petroleum refining and marketing giant BPCL, is a harbinger of what is to come. The government has announced that it plans to hawk virtually all public sector assets in the coming period. As elsewhere worldwide, these sales will necessarily be at distress prices, thereby ensuring the "success" of the privatization program.

There is a peculiar but significant feature of India's version of the "austerity"-driven asset-stripping program. Elsewhere, the native rulers have almost always dragged their feet, refused at first to submit to certain clauses, and even put up a temporary show of defiance. This is because almost all such countries have been forced to submit in the face of a sudden foreign exchange crisis. Their submission to the "austerity" program is marked by political turmoil, as people resist their country's subjugation and expropriation.

By contrast, India is not facing an *immediate* foreign exchange crisis (though the possibility is always present). Rather, the rulers themselves have come forward aggressively with the package of "austerity" and "reforms" as *their own*. Even more outlandishly, they have promoted it as "self-reliance."

Inadequate and Misleading Explanations of Foreign Capital's Opposition to Government Spending

For three decades now, the IMF, and now the foreign credit ratings agencies, warned the Indian government about the size of its *fiscal deficit* (the sum of all borrowing by the government in a given year) and called for government spending to be reduced. They continue to raise the alarm in the midst of the present grave crisis. There are several intertwined reasons why foreign investors in India oppose an expansion of government spending. But before getting to this, let us first address some of the explanations that are usually given, which are misleading or incomplete.

1. "Foreign Investors Are Worried About Inflation"

No doubt, foreign investors are in general worried about inflation in India (and countries like India). Inflation, they fear, would cause the rupee's exchange rate to the dollar/euro/yen to fall. This would wipe out part or all of the financial gains made by foreign investors on their Indian investments when they convert back to the dollar or other international currencies (see endnote 98 for explanation).[98]

However, with incomes collapsing, there is no threat of demand-pull inflation. Even the government's chief economic advisor acknowledges that there is no generalized threat of inflation, but rather of *deflation*—that is, falling prices due to the evaporation of demand.[99] Demand is depressed because people do not have money to spend; so much so that, even though the supply of many commodities was disrupted or blocked, prices (even of essentials such as food) by and large did not rise correspondingly. Demand is also very depressed internationally, as reflected in the price of oil and other commodities, further depressing domestic prices.

Had food been in short supply, an increase in government spending might have triggered inflation, as food production cannot be ramped up on short notice. But, in fact, the government had vast excess stocks of foodgrains on hand in March and a good harvest was anticipated in April. In fact, the imminent threat was the opposite—that a collapse of demand would cause a fall in the prices received by peasants.

No doubt, the prices of specific commodities may rise if the supply chain is disrupted because of the lockdown. However, in such circumstances, the government would need to ensure supply through its own direct action. This would require additional government spending. If the government failed to spend in such a situation, it would actually aggravate such individual pockets of price raises.

Rather than demand-pull inflation, we are witnessing *cost-push* inflation: a rise in the cost of inputs. The source of this threat is not government spending, but government taxation—the decision to raise taxes steeply on petroleum products. This is a straightforward squeezing of the poor, since petroleum enters indirectly into the production of every good. Such taxes on consumption take away a greater proportion of the income of the poor than they do of the rich. Unsurprisingly, foreign investors do not oppose such measures.

In brief, the reason foreign investors oppose government spending in India at present cannot be out of fear of inflation.

2. "Foreign Investors Are Worried About the Size of the Government Debt"

This is another red herring. First, India's government debt is overwhelmingly held by Indians, and hence need not be a concern to foreign investors. (In fact, perhaps four-fifths of government debt is held by entities owned or controlled by the government itself—public sector banks, public sector insurance firms, the RBI, and provident funds.) The great bulk of liabilities to foreign investors are owed by Indian corporate firms, not by the government.

Second, the relevant figure to assess the sustainability of government debt is not its absolute level, but the ratio of government debt to GDP, since a larger GDP can generate more tax revenues for the government to make payments on the debt. As it happens, India's government debt to GDP ratio has been lower in recent years than in the early 2000s (see Chart 1 for data on the combined debt of central and state governments).

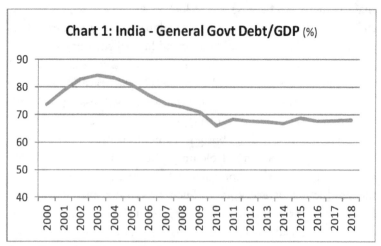

Chart 1: India - General Govt Debt/GDP (%)

Source: International Monetary Fund.

Third, *if the government fails to spend adequately, GDP will shrink. In this case, even if government debt were to stay at the same level, the government debt to GDP ratio would worsen.* Something along these lines is likely to happen now, as India's GDP shrinks in 2020 and 2021.

To take a hypothetical example, say that in Year 1 government debt is 72 percent of GDP and the government projects that in Year 2 GDP will rise in nominal terms (meaning, real growth plus inflation) by 10 percent. Let us assume that, in an effort to keep down its debt, the government decides to limit its spending and caps the increase in its borrowings at 8 percent of GDP in Year 2. If nominal GDP were to grow just as the government projects, the government debt to GDP ratio would hardly increase.

However, if, in our example, some event were to take place that deals the economy a huge blow, the level of government spending could turn out to be too meagre to ensure growth and the economy could slip into a recession. Let us say that, as a result, the GDP shrinks 10 percent in real terms in Year 2, and even the nominal GDP (including inflation) winds up 6 percent lower than the previous year. In this case, the same debt burden would shoot up to 90 percent of GDP because GDP is lower, which in turn is because government spending did not boost demand adequately. That is, the debt to GDP ratio in this case deteriorates inordinately because *spending is too low* in the present situation. (This is what happened, for example, in Greece.)

Yet, foreign investors ignore this and oppose any sizable increase in government spending, even in a depression.

Fourth, if foreign investors are for some reason obsessed with the growth of government debt, it should be obvious to them that there are two ways to curb government borrowing: reduce spending or raise tax revenues. Indeed, India's government spending, as a percentage of its GDP, is low compared to comparable countries. The problem is that India's tax revenues and GDP are low too, compelling the government to borrow.[100] In the period of neoliberalism, income inequality in India has risen to levels not seen since British rule and its wealth inequalities are even steeper.[101] Despite this, foreign investors press only for reducing spending.

Besides, within tax revenues, there are broadly two ways to raise tax revenues: taxes on goods and services, which are paid by all, or taxes on income, which are paid by the better off. Thus, there is a clear division of class interests in deciding how to bridge the fiscal deficit. Foreign investors support taxes on goods and services, which are mostly paid for by the vast majority of people, but are vehemently opposed to increasing taxes on the incomes of corporations and wealthier individuals.

Why? Because (1) they too would have to pay taxes on income; (2) much of foreign investment caters to elite markets, so foreign investors are in favor of income concentration as this expands the market for their goods, whereas taxation of income is generally progressive (that is, it reduces inequality); and (3) concentration of income in the hands of the top 5 to 10 percent buoys the share market (those who hold shares, directly or through mutual funds, fall within the top 10 percent), and thereby increases the price of shares owned by foreign investors.

From this it is crystal clear that foreign investors are not concerned with the government debt as such. It is merely an excuse for them to apply pressure for reduction of government spending.

A recent incident reveals how acutely sensitive the government is to the concerns of foreign investors. On their own initiative, a group of Indian Revenue Service officers prepared a report on the government's fiscal options in response to COVID-19, suggesting some (very moderate) increases in taxation of the rich.[102] Far from appreciating their patriotic efforts, the government reacted with alarm and vindictiveness: it condemned the report, opened an inquiry against fifty junior officers, and charged three senior officers, relieving them of their posts. As justification, the authorities claimed that "the report created panic and tax policy uncertainty in the already stressed economic conditions in the country."[103]

3. "Foreign Investors Are Ideologically Opposed to the Public Sector and Government Spending"

This statement has an element of truth. Part of neoliberalism is its elaborate ideological edifice, including notions about the "free market," "individualism," "dynamism of private enterprise," "inefficiency of the public sector," "removing distortions in the market," and so on, which cast a spell over many intellectuals. Such propositions, however bogus they may be, form the very frame of thinking of most economists today: they have been trained in them, they practice them continuously, and they do not conceive of anything beyond them.

Nevertheless, the ideological framework, at best, explains the thinking of economists, but does not adequately explain the conduct of foreign investors. If powerful business interests are ideologically opposed to something, that begs the question: What attracts them to this particular ideology, since they keenly calculate the financial costs and benefits of every policy? Moreover, whenever international capital finds any cherished ideological tenet to be in conflict with its cold hard profits, it discards the tenet without much ado. This is apparent during each crisis, such as the Great Financial Crisis of 2007–09 or the present COVID-19 crisis. The world's richest countries, led by the United States, jack up their fiscal deficits dramatically—10, 15, 20 percent of GDP—until the economy recovers. After it does recover, they go back to preaching the virtues of austerity.

Thus, ideology cannot fundamentally explain the opposition of foreign investors to government spending in India and other "underdeveloped" countries.

THE REAL REASONS FOR FOREIGN INVESTORS' OPPOSITION

A regime of austerity in government spending, while ruinous for a particular economy, can yield rich returns for foreign investors. The following are not distinct points but different aspects of the same theme.

1. When a government refuses to spend and revive demand, economic growth depends entirely on the desire of private sector investors to invest. In order to stimulate the private corporate sector to do so, rulers provide all sorts of inducements and subsidies at the cost of the people. During a crisis, the bounties get even more extravagant.

Such gifts to the private corporate sector benefit foreign investors, whether through their local subsidiaries, their ties with local firms, or through their purchase of shares in local firms.

2. Similarly, when governments are under pressure to reduce their fiscal deficits, they carry out "reforms" that create opportunities for private profit making, albeit at a cost to the public. For example, when governments cut back on infrastructural investment, as well as public health services, education, agricultural extension services, and other social and economic services, they correspondingly expand opportunities for private infrastructure firms, private corporate health care, private schools and universities, corporate penetration of agriculture, and so on. In pursuit of this aim, India for some years became the world's leader in public-private partnerships. These have resulted in massive fiascos and scandals at a staggering loss to the public, but they remain the government's preferred method of providing public services.

3. Furthermore, under the banner of reducing the fiscal deficit, governments sell shares in profitable public sector firms or sell off the firms outright. Since governments are selling these assets under the pressure of time and budgetary targets, they sell them in "fire sales," that is, at distress prices. These create bonanzas for cash-rich foreign investors.

We have recently seen a living demonstration of all the above three points, with the finance minister's marathon presentation of the government's economic package 'for COVID-19.' The package contains government *spending* worth hardly 1 percent of GDP; but under the cover of addressing the crisis, it brings in a staggering list of privatizations, deregulations, and other gifts to the corporate sector and foreign investors. As we mentioned in the earlier chapter, when foreign investors oppose an expansion of government expenditure, the government banks solely on stimulating the appetite of capitalists to invest, by providing them incentives and concessions of all types. This the present government has again turned to with gusto.

4. Finally, slashing government spending depresses domestic demand. That depresses the prices of assets and labor power in the country.

It may also lead to domestic firms making losses and defaulting on their loans. In these conditions, foreign investors can buy up various assets, including debt-stressed Indian private firms, at distress prices. (In fact, a section of the large corporate sector in India itself appears worried about this and has been asking the government to increase its spending and boost demand.)

In times of worldwide crisis, governments of the developed world expand their spending dramatically, even as governments of underdeveloped countries like India (or even relatively weaker capitalist countries like Greece) put government spending on a starvation diet. In this situation, corporations of the developed world are even better equipped to raid underdeveloped countries for their distressed assets.

What this means is that, *even though the crisis reduces "regular" profits for international capital, it is also an opportunity to make extraordinary windfall gains.* Thus, prolonging or deepening the crisis in underdeveloped or weak countries and exercising tight control over government policies in those countries can yield bonanzas to international capital.

EXAMPLES OF HOW FOREIGN FINANCE MAKES USE OF A CRISIS IN WEAK AND SUBORDINATE COUNTRIES

In the endnote "Financial Crisis as Opportunity for Foreign Investors," we take three examples of how foreign finance uses a crisis in a weak or subordinate country to extract gains for itself. Although the three examples of South Korea, Thailand, and Greece are striking, they are also fairly representative, and many more instances could be cited.

In fact, the 1997–98 Asian financial crisis spanned a number of countries with widely differing economies. All these countries had recently liberalized their economies, received substantial inflows of foreign capital, and, at this juncture, were hit by outflows of foreign capital in rapid succession. They turned to the IMF for emergency loans. The IMF used the crisis to engineer a foreign (in particular, U.S.) financial invasion of these economies.

In the case of **South Korea**, which had a fiscal surplus, the IMF nevertheless insisted on fiscal cuts and high interest rates. The ensuing economic crash was the predictable and *planned* outcome of this program. The IMF demanded the breakup of Korea's distinctive business conglomerates (the *chaebol*) that controlled the economy, so as to allow scope for the expansion of foreign capital; labor market "flexibility" (large-scale retrenchments and the replacement of permanent labor with temporary workers, who receive lower wages and have no security); and freedom for foreign investors in the share market and direct investment, including hostile takeovers of Korean firms. A massive transfer of Korean assets into foreign hands ensued. Major Korean firms—Samsung, POSCO, Hyundai—became majority foreign owned, as did the bulk of the banking sector. The sale of Korean assets, whether private or government owned, took place at distress prices. Since foreign investors alone were flush with funds, they won the jackpot. Meanwhile, small firms folded, the working class was informalized, and inequality rose.

All these measures were implemented in **Thailand**, with the same results. As in South Korea, so too in Thailand did the United States and its intellectual entourage blame what they called "crony capitalism" for the crisis. A sizable share of Thai industry and the dominant part of the financial sector came under foreign control. Sections of the Thai big bourgeoisie who had earlier taken large foreign loans, but now tried to retain control of their firms during the crisis, sank; those who adjusted to a changed role, as gateways for foreign capital, survived—even flourished.

Greece's economy had grown rapidly in the period before the Global Financial Crisis of 2007–09, as had its government deficits and foreign borrowings. The main sources of its foreign debt were banks within the European Union (EU), in Germany, France, and the United Kingdom. A market panic was *engineered* in 2010 regarding the size of Greece's public debt, after which Greece was unable to borrow internationally and had to turn to the IMF and EU for a bailout. The alternative—for Greece to default, leave the EU, and revive its own (pre-euro) currency—would have opened up the path for Greece's eventual recovery. This was hurriedly preempted by the IMF-EU "bailout" of 2010, ensuring Greece adhered to the path laid down by international capital.

As conditions for this and two further "bailouts," the IMF, EU, and European Central Bank imposed on Greece drastic cuts in government expenditure, mass retrenchments, increases in consumption tax, and privatizations. These caused a catastrophic and predictable shrinkage of the Greek economy. However, the public debt did not decline, but slightly rose. More importantly, the debt to GDP ratio rose by over 50 percent, because GDP itself shrank by more than one-fifth. There is no foreseeable exit for Greece from debt and its associated conditions, stretching four decades into the future. Unemployment has soared, wages have fallen, and poverty has shot up.

It is a fiction that Greece's privatization program can reduce its public debt. IMF data show privatization has reduced the public debt by 1.3 percent between 2008 and 2018 and will reduce it another 1.2 percent between 2019 and 2028. The proceeds of privatization are at any rate depressed by the fact that public assets are being sold at distressed prices, at financial gunpoint, during a worldwide economic decline. State-owned enterprises, infrastructure (including thirty-five ports, forty airports, and the natural gas company), buildings, three thousand pieces of real estate, national monuments, national roads, and the military industry are all up for grabs. The deals are a scandal, such as when the Frankfurt Airport led to Fraport consortium's takeover of Greece's fourteen busiest regional airports, major tourism hubs, for €1.23 billion.

A few general observations, in telegraphic form, on the basis of the examples in the endnote, "Financial Crisis as Opportunity for Foreign Investors":

1. These economies were rendered vulnerable precisely by the large inflows of capital they received in the wake of further liberalization or their integration into the global economy.
2. The three economies described were not typical debtor countries. They were classified as middle to high income: South Korea and

Greece are members of the rich nations' club, the Organisation for Economic Co-operation and Development; Greece is a member of the North Atlantic Treaty Organization; South Korea houses thirty-six thousand U.S. troops; Thailand was a military ally of the United States at the time. Despite this, their economies were thrown into crisis and they were ruthlessly stripped of their assets. Other weaker economies like India can assess their own chances from the fate of these three countries.

3. When the crisis arrived, the ruling classes of South Korea, Thailand, and Greece simply transferred their foreign liabilities to the people—they became a debt for the people to work off. Imperialism overnight invented myths to justify its rapacious attack: "crony capitalism" in Asia, "lazy/pampered/overpaid workers" in Greece, and "statistical fraud" in Greece as well.

4. Once the crisis arrived, an austerity regime was immediately imposed by the IMF and other institutions. This regime was designed to prolong and deepen the crisis, and to take away any instruments by which the economy could recover. Government spending was placed under tight restraint.

There is a noteworthy difference between East Asia and Greece. After 1997, the world economy experienced a revival. In particular, the Asian economies, more integrated with the rapidly growing Chinese economy, recovered and grew rapidly (albeit in a more distorted way). By contrast, after 2008, the world economy did not experience a *real* revival. Within this, there was no scope for the Greek economy to recover even in a more subjugated form. Any economy now going into a crisis of this type will find it harder to achieve full recovery; it might even shrink permanently, as Greece did.

5. Once the crisis set in, the native ruling classes of the affected countries haggled, to some extent, for extra time, but they ultimately threw in their lot with foreign capital and adjusted their operations to its tighter grip. The ruling-class sections that adjusted better to their modified role survived, even flourished.

6. The agent institutions—the IMF, EU, European Central Bank, and

credit ratings agencies—used the foreign liabilities of these econo-mies as a lever with which to pry them open and separate them from their precious assets.

7. The entire process effected a large-scale transfer of domestic assets to imperialism. Various elements of the domestic economy, such as labor, small firms, the public sector, and even the large corporate sector, were extensively restructured in favor of foreign capital.

8. Imperialism does not necessarily have a stake in reviving pro-ductive activity. Particularly in its present phase, uncertain of the prospects for long-term growth, its cannibalistic aspects come to the fore. Hence, it has used these crises, indeed prolonged and deepened them, to pick off the targeted economies.

9. People resisted, defended their rights as workers and working people, and defended their country's sovereignty in doing so. In certain places, they even unseated the native rulers. But, due to the weakness or absence of political forces grounded among the masses that truly represented the people's interests, ruling classes and imperialism were able to restore their grip.

With these observations in mind, let us turn to India.

India's Credit Boom and Bust

There are certain similarities between India and the crisis-hit countries we have just described. These arise from (1) the role of international finance in fueling the pattern of growth experienced in their "boom" periods, and (2) the regimes of austerity and deflation put in place thereafter, and the consequent transfer of the country's assets to for-eign investors.

The Boom

As R. Nagaraj puts it, India's "dream run" of 2003–08 "was, in fact, a typical credit boom, with its source of finance sowing the seeds of its own destruction."[104] To draw on his account, as the advanced economies expanded credit massively starting in 2002, capital flows from these economies to "emerging markets" more than doubled from 2002 to 2007. In India, foreign capital inflows soared to 10 percent of GDP by 2007–08, the peak of India's boom.

Less than one-fourth of foreign flows were absorbed by investment. However, they played a larger role in triggering the boom. As foreign capital flowed in, the banking system was flush with funds.[105] Banks now liberally lent to a range of borrowers from infrastructure investors to apartment buyers. The ratio of bank credit to GDP rose from 35 percent in 2002–03 to 50 percent in 2007–08.

Easy inflows of foreign capital fueled bank credit at low interest rates. Foreign investment in the share market led to share prices soaring, enabling companies to raise capital cheaply through new share issues.[106] The private corporate sector more readily took on risky investments and speculative land purchases. The ratio of profit after tax to net worth of firms doubled, from 9.1 percent in 2002–03 to 18.2 percent in 2006–07.

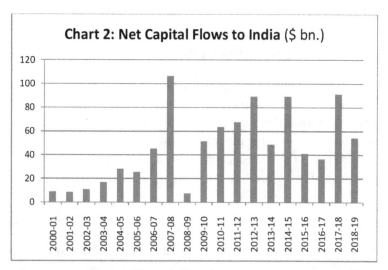

Source: Reserve Bank of India, *Handbook of Statistics on the Indian Economy, 2018–19* (Mumbai: Reserve Bank of India, 2019).

With the government encouraging public-private partnerships by the corporate sector with loans from public sector banks, the share of infrastructure (power, telecoms, and roads) in bank credit rose from 9 percent in 2003 to 33.5 percent in 2011. At the same time, credit fueled a boom in the consumerism of better-off sections, with the share of personal loans (for housing, automobiles, and consumer durables) in bank credit nearly doubling between 2000–01 and 2005–06. The pattern of production was skewed even further to elite markets rather than mass consumption. Rapid growth reinforced the prevailing belief that India was at a "take-off" stage and the endemic problem of demand was now a thing of the past. The government's *Economic Survey 2016–17* looked back on this period thus:

> Firms . . . launched new projects worth lakhs of crores [trillions of rupees], particularly in infrastructure-related areas such as power generation, steel, and telecoms, setting off the biggest investment boom in the country's history. . . . This investment was financed by an astonishing credit boom, also the largest in the nation's history, one that was sizeable even compared to other large credit booms internationally. In the span of just three years, running from 2004–05 to 2008–09, the amount of non-food bank credit doubled. And this was just the credit from banks: there were also large inflows of funding from overseas. . . . All of this added up to an extraordinary increase in the debt of non-financial corporations.[107]

Accumulation Through Grabbing Public Assets, Subsidies and Natural Resources

As the prospects of rapid accumulation of wealth whetted the appetites of large capitalists, they turned to the public sector banks for loans and the government for all sorts of assistance. The boom was thus further fueled by a massive private grab of public assets, government subsidies, and natural resources (which are not really amenable to being valued in money terms, since they cannot be replaced) in the name of infrastructure. India was the world leader in public-private partnerships between 2006 and 2012. By the end of December 2012, it had over nine hundred public-private partnership projects in the infrastructure sector, at different stages of implementation. But this growth in public-private partnerships was birthmarked with scandal—thus, private airports, coal mining (power), and natural gas exploration have been the subjects of critical reports by the comptroller and auditor general.

More generally, the private pillage of natural resources during the "boom" later was manifested in a number of scandals: the manipulation of allocations of radio frequencies for mobile services; illegal mining of iron ore and its export; large-scale land acquisitions for special economic zones in the name of industrial activity, but actually for the purpose of real estate; stalled public-private partnership road projects; and so on. An important aspect of these deals was that, by systematically overstating ("gold plating") the project cost and borrowing the major portion of these overstated costs from public sector banks, many private promoters actually invested no money of their own in the projects. A Reserve Bank deputy governor said that the funding for the public-private partnerships had come from the public sector banks, rather than the promoters' pockets, to such an extent that "the 'Public-Private partnership' has, in effect, remained a 'Public only' venture."[108] Gajendra Haldea, at the time principal advisor to the Planning Commission on infrastructure and public-private partnerships, states:

> Financing of gold-plated costs, reckless disbursement of funds, irresponsible waiver of conditionalities, bypassing of contract terms, lack of any worthwhile stake of the project sponsors and diversion of funds became the principal attributes of PSB [public sector-bank] lending to infrastructure projects. This was brought out in a Discussion Paper titled "Sub Prime Highways" circulated by the author in June 2010. However, given the inconvenient facts stated in that paper, it was ignored, perhaps deliberately, by the relevant Ministries as well as the PSBs. This story was

reinforced in another Discussion Paper titled "Infrastructure: A Policy Logjam" that was brought out by the author in June 2013, but this too was overlooked.[109]

Haldea demonstrates that private road projects were gold plated an average of 90 percent over the actual project cost. He estimates that "haircuts" (write offs) and budgetary support amounting to ₹6 trillion ($100 billion at the time of his estimate) would be required to restore the health of public sector banks and other financial institutions that had lent to such infrastructure projects.

Since these assets and funds have been alienated from the Indian public, it would stand to reason that, when these private promoters later failed to service their debt, the assets should have come into the hands of the public and the authorities should have relentlessly pursued private owners for the return of funds, including by expropriating their entire property and arresting them. However, what happens instead is a *second* alienation of public assets, as we shall see.

The Global Financial Crisis and the Two Phases of the Fiscal Deficit

In 2008, the Global Financial Crisis put a sudden stop to foreign inflows. Credit froze and growth slumped, worldwide and in India. However, the world's leading economies, whose own financial sectors were endangered, quickly came together to revive global growth. They allowed, even encouraged, the weaker economies and third world countries to expand their government spending for about two years, approximately India's fiscal years 2008–09 and 2009–10. In those two years, the central government's fiscal deficit soared from 2.5 percent of GDP to 6.5 percent (see chart 3).

In the chart of GDP growth (Chart 4), we can mark different phases.

1. From about 2003, there was a surge in growth. With large capital inflows and a credit boom, private investment and consumption powered growth. The government's fiscal deficits (see Chart 3) meanwhile fell to just 2.5 percent at the height of the growth

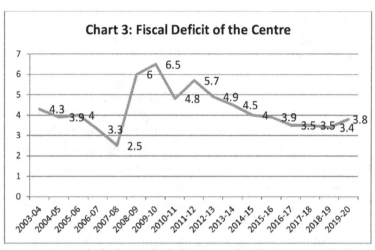

Source: Reserve Bank of India, *Handbook of Statistics on the Indian Economy, 2018–19,* and Union Budget documents.

boom—which, as is often the case in such booms, came just before the fall.

2. In 2008–09, with the Global Financial Crisis, GDP growth slumped.

3. However, the government expanded the fiscal deficit and bank lending in 2008–09 and 2009–10, which (with a slight lag) led to growth reviving in 2009–10 and 2010–11.

4. At that point, the international environment once more turned hostile to public spending. The government started reducing expenditure and growth slowed again. (The picture is a bit confused due to the government's new series of GDP, with the base year 2011–12, which overstates GDP growth due to its dubious methods. But even this series shows growth in gross value added falling from 2016–17 onward and finally landing at 3.9 percent growth in 2019–20, that is, the same level as 2002–03.)

Why Did Growth Slow Post-Global Financial Crisis Despite Inflows?

One question arises from charts 2, 3, and 4. As we saw, between 2003 and 2008, inflows of foreign capital fueled rapid GDP growth.

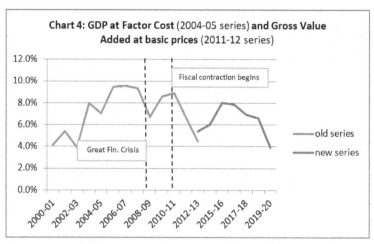

Chart 4: GDP at Factor Cost (2004-05 series) and Gross Value Added at basic prices (2011-12 series)

Source: National Statistical Office. Gross domestic product at factor cost in 2004–05 series; gross value added at basic prices in 2011–12 series. ("GDP at factor cost" in the old series has been renamed "Gross Value Added at basic prices" in the new series.)

They did so despite declining government fiscal deficits. Yet, in the period *after* the Global Financial Crisis, while fiscal deficits no doubt declined, India once again received large capital inflows. In fact, the average for 2009–10 to 2018–19 was $63.4 billion a year, considerably higher than the average for 2003–08, which was $44.4 billion a year. Why then did the second round of inflows not spark the same growth boom as the first?

There are three reasons, in our view. First, the global economy never really recovered from the Global Financial Crisis. The biggest beneficiaries of the huge financial packages in the developed world were the financial sectors of those countries. Meanwhile, the world economy was burdened with a huge accumulation of debt and slowed sharply. In particular, the third world ("emerging markets") had slumped drastically. Indeed, the world was poised to reenter a recession even before COVID-19, due to causes internal to and inherent in its pattern of development.

Second, it is partly an illusion that India's rapid growth of 2003–08 took place amid falling fiscal deficits. After all, private corporate investment during this period was funded by *public sector* banks.

Instead of the government itself borrowing (that is, incurring a fiscal deficit) for infrastructure, government-owned banks provided loans to the private corporate sector to set up infrastructure. The losses on that would eventually have to be borne by the government, in the form of recapitalizing the banks that had lent to the private firms. Thus, by encouraging risky, publicly funded private investment in infrastructure in the 2003–08 period, the government was incurring a postponed fiscal deficit, which simply came onto the government's books in the later period when the private firms defaulted.

Third, and more basically, the rapid growth of 2003–08 was bound to slow at some point precisely because it was not a "new normal" but a *bubble*. The endemic problem of demand in the Indian economy had to come to the fore once again. Given the poverty of the Indian masses, they did not constitute an attractive market for big capital. The boom was thus skewed heavily toward elite demand, but the growth of this demand could not be sustained endlessly. The types of economic, social, and political changes required to bring about widespread increases in income and demand, and to reorient production to cater to that demand, were nowhere on the horizon. Instead, the rulers continued to move aggressively in the opposite direction, destroying livelihoods on a large scale, depressing wages, and concentrating wealth. Hence, the boom was fated to peter out.

After 2010, the picture of slowing growth and continuing large capital inflows demonstrated in the charts implies *a growing burden of foreign liabilities on the weakening economic base of our country*. This contradiction must at some point be resolved: either through the repudiation of foreign liabilities, which will not happen under the existing social order, or through Indian assets getting transferred to foreign hands.

The Rajan Regime of Demand Suppression

In May and June 2013, the U.S. central bank, the Federal Reserve, began talking of gradually reducing the flood of money supply it had unleashed to tackle the 2007–09 crisis. Developing countries had received a share of capital inflows due to that earlier policy, boosting their growth. The signs that it would be reversed soon set off a panic, with capital flows halting, external borrowing rates rising, exchange rates depreciating, and share markets falling. India was suddenly listed among the "fragile five" economies (along with Brazil, South Africa, Turkey, and Indonesia) prone to shocks as the United States tapered off its earlier measures.

In this situation, former chief economist of the IMF, Raghuram Rajan, was appointed governor of the RBI. In his first statement as governor (September 4, 2013), Rajan asserted that the primary role of the central bank was to keep prices low, whatever the reason for a rise in the price level. He then set about instituting measures to bring down inflation by depressing the incomes of peasants and other small producers, as well as workers' wages.

Rajan set up an "expert committee" to prepare a monetary policy framework for the RBI (and, thereby, for the government). The committee's report asserted the need to constrain the government from spending. If the government increased demand by spending, the central bank would have to suppress demand by jacking up interest rates. The class nature of this inflation control became clear very rapidly. The report specifically criticized measures such as rural employment schemes and the Food Security Act:

The Government must set a path of fiscal consolidation with zero or few escape clauses; ideally this should be legislated and publicly communicated.... Furthermore, it may be important to identify and address other fiscal/ administrative sources of pressure on inflation/drivers of inflation persistence. For instance, the design of programmes like Mahatma Gandhi National Rural Employment Guarantee Act (MGNREGA) provide a sustained upward push to nominal wages unrelated to productivity growth, and the National Food Security Act which could increase demand for foodgrains without corresponding efforts to augment supply. A policy induced wage-price/cost-price spiral can be damaging for the credibility of an inflation targeting framework. *The*

burden on monetary policy to compensate for these sources of infla-
tion pressure is correspondingly higher.[110]

A Monetary Policy Committee was set up with the sole target
of keeping the inflation rate around 4 percent. Inflation came down
steadily, trumpeted as an achievement of the RBI and the government.[111] However, since the incomes of working people actually fell in
this period, whom did "inflation targeting" actually serve? It served the
medium-term interests of predatory *foreign capital*: demand shrank
and the price of Indian assets was further and further depressed.

Non-Performing Assets: Offspring of the Bubble

Rajan's next major project concerned the bad debts, particularly the
large debts owed to the banks by the corporate sector. Before we get
to Rajan's actions, let us describe the background.

In the period before Modi's election in 2014, the corporate media
had argued that the reason for the slump in the economy was "policy
paralysis" and the stalling of environmental clearances for industrial
and mining projects. The *Economic Survey 2014–15*, however, punc-
tured this:

> Perhaps contrary to popular belief, the evidence points towards
> *over exuberance and a credit bubble as primary reasons (rather*
> *than lack of regulatory clearances) for stalled projects in the pri-*
> *vate sector.* . . . An unambiguous fact emerging from the data is
> that the debt to equity for Indian non-financial corporates has
> been rising at a fairly alarming rate over time and is significantly
> higher when viewed against other comparator countries. . . .
>
> Tying things together . . . suggests that *Indian firms face a*
> *classic debt overhang problem in the aftermath of a debt fuelled*
> *investment bubble.*[112]

The *Economic Survey 2016–17* described the descent into the corporate non-performing assets crisis and its scale:

Forecast revenues collapsed after the GFC [Global Financial Crisis]; projects that had been built around the assumption that growth would continue at double-digit levels were suddenly confronted with growth rates half that level. As if these problems were not enough, financing costs increased sharply. Firms that borrowed domestically suffered when the RBI increased interest rates to quell double-digit inflation. And firms that had borrowed abroad when the rupee was trading around Rs 40/dollar were hit hard when the rupee depreciated, forcing them to repay their debts at exchange rates closer to Rs 60–70/dollar....

By 2013, nearly one-third of corporate debt was owed by companies with an interest coverage ratio less than 1 ("IC1 companies") [meaning they did not earn enough to pay the interest obligations on their loans], many of them in the infrastructure (especially power generation) and metals sectors. By 2015, the share of IC1 companies reached nearly 40 percent.[113]

This was followed by the drama of "restructuring" corporate debt:

Accordingly, banks decided to give stressed enterprises more time by postponing loan repayments, restructuring by 2014–15 no less than 6.4 percent of their loans outstanding. They also extended fresh funding to the stressed firms to tide them over until demand recovered.

As a result, total stressed assets have far exceeded the headline figure of NPAs [non-performing assets]. To that amount one needs to add the restructured loans, as well as the loans owed by IC1 companies that have not even been recognised as problem debts – the ones that have been "evergreened", where banks lend firms the money needed to pay their interest obligations. Market analysts estimate that the unrecognised debts are around 4 percent of gross loans, and perhaps 5 percent at public sector banks. In that case, *total stressed assets would amount to about 16.6 percent of banking system loans—and nearly 20 percent of loans at the [government-owned] state banks.* ...

[Further,] aggregate cash flow in the stressed companies—
which even in 2014 wasn't sufficient to service their debts—has
fallen by roughly 40 percent in less than two years.

These companies have consequently had to borrow considerable amounts in order to continue their operations. Debts of the
top 10 stressed corporate groups, in particular, have increased
at an extraordinarily rapid rate, essentially tripling in the last
six years. As this has occurred, their interest obligations have
climbed rapidly. . . .

At the same time, corporate stress seems to be spreading.
For much of the period since the Global Financial Crisis, the
problems were concentrated in the large companies which had
taken on excessive leverage during the mid-2000s boom, while
the more cautious smaller and midsize companies had by and
large continued to service their debts. Starting in the second half
of 2016, however, a significant proportion of the increases in
NPAs—four-fifths of the slippages during the second quarter—
came from mid-size and MSMEs [micro, small, and medium
enterprises], as smaller companies that had been suffering from
poor sales and profitability for a number of years struggled to
remain current on their debts.[114]

In fact, the crisis spread *from* large firms *to* smaller ones. One way
this happened was that larger firms simply did not pay their dues to
small and medium enterprises.

As the economy slowed further after 2011 and the revenues from
public-private partnership projects appeared less attractive, private
investors stopped work on these projects. The number of new public-
private partnership projects in India, which had been the highest in
the world between 2008 and 2012, fell to low levels within a few years
and continue to languish.[115]

Despite extensive "restructuring" of corporate debt, the borrowing firms were not able to revive their financial position, presumably
because the bulk of such investments were risky or unsound in the
first place. Between August and November 2015, the RBI carried out

Chart 5: NPA as Percent of Gross Advances, Scheduled Commercial Banks

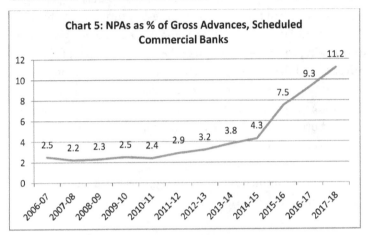

Chart 5: NPAs as % of Gross Advances, Scheduled Commercial Banks

Source: Reserve Bank of India, *Handbook of Statistics on the Indian Economy, 2018–19.*

a special inspection of the banks and found that they were using various means to avoid classifying many loans as "non-performing" (that is, in default). Rajan talked tough and told the banks to reclassify the loans by March 2016. This led to an immediate surge in banks' non-performing assets.

Here, we need to distinguish between responsibility for a phenomenon and the agenda behind tackling that phenomenon in a certain way. Clearly, the Indian large capitalist class was responsible for the phenomenon of corporate sector non-performing assets, with the encouragement of foreign finance and the critical help of the Indian state. What was required in response to the non-performing assets phenomenon was the nationalization of all the assets involved (which were already publicly funded) and the relentless pursuit of corporate defaulters for the recovery of diverted funds. By contrast, Rajan's sudden decision to crack down by classifying a much larger number of corporate debts as non-performing assets was not part of any such national developmental agenda. Rather, it subtly advanced a different goal, one that would ultimately benefit not the Indian public, but foreign financial investors.

A major step forward in this process was the legislation of an Insolvency and Bankruptcy Code in 2016. Before this, beginning in the 1980s, there had been a number of restructuring and rehabilitation schemes for the debts of firms, but in practice these largely helped the borrowing corporate firms retain their hold and divert funds. The Insolvency and Bankruptcy Code, by contrast, enforces a timebound process in which the creditors, not the debtor firm, are in control. The creditors appoint "insolvency professionals" who take over the assets and bring about a speedy "resolution," most often the sale of the asset to other investors. Successive RBI circulars have made the process even tighter. In 2018, the government announced that over 2,500 cases of insolvency had been brought before the newly formed National Company Law Tribunal.

Buildup of External Commercial Borrowings

A further source of vulnerability for the Indian corporate sector is the rise of corporate dependence on foreign debt. This was in part a fallout of the corporate funding crunch domestically. After the Global Financial Crisis, India's corporate sector turned even more heavily to external commercial borrowings (ECBs). These increased from 27.1 percent of India's external debt in 2010 to 39.7 percent in at the end of December 2019, at which point they stood at $223.8 billion.

In 2016, the RBI had tightened regulations regarding ECBs in a number of ways, among them requiring that borrowers "hedge" their external borrowings 100 percent. (*Hedging* means to buy a special financial contract which protects you against the risk of a change in a particular price. In this case, since ECBs would have to be repaid in dollars or other such currencies, and there is a risk that the rupee might fall more than anticipated vis-à-vis the dollar, the borrower might have to pay back more rupees than anticipated, leading to a crisis. A *hedge* in such a situation would be a financial contract that promises the buyer more returns if the rupee depreciates against the dollar. In this way, the losses on the original contract would be cancelled out partly or wholly by the hedge contract. Such

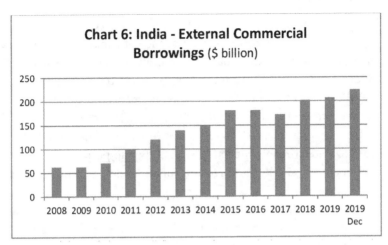

Chart 6: India - External Commercial Borrowings ($ billion)

Source: Ministry of Finance. All figures are for the end of March 2020, unless otherwise specified.

contracts, which are a form of insurance, are sold every day on financial markets.) As a result of the RBI's more restrictive regulations and tightened monitoring, the flow of ECBs temporarily dropped.

In 2018, however, the government put pressure on the RBI to relax ECBs once again, in order to give relief to the corporate sector as well as to attract more foreign inflows. The RBI provided the requested relaxations, allowing ECBs with only 70 percent hedging in place of 100 percent hedging. Private corporate borrowers took to ECBs once more with gusto, and between January and December 2019 ECBs rose by $29 billion.

It is also quite likely that some firms did not hedge 70 percent or did not hedge at all, and the RBI decided to wink at this. According to the chief economist of CARE Ratings, which published a study on the rise in ECBs, a hedge would cost 4 to 4.5 percent, thus many companies borrowed without any cover, betting on a stable exchange rate.[116]

In particular, there was a surge of borrowing by the financial services sector—banks, non-banking financial corporations, housing finance companies, and mutual funds. In the wake of the September 2018 collapse of the mammoth non-banking financial corporation

Infrastructure Leasing & Financial Services Limited and the crisis in Dewan Housing Finance, the confidence of banks and investors was shaken. Non-banking financial corporations were unable to raise funds from domestic banks and capital markets. To ease the problem, the RBI opened the door for non-banking financial corporations to borrow through ECBs. In July 2019, the RBI relaxed the uses to which ECBs could be put and allowed borrowers to use these funds for working capital requirements, general corporate purposes, and the repayment of rupee loans. Borrowing for on-lending by non-banking financial corporations was also permitted.

This implies that the financial sector, which holds claims on a large number of debtor firms, is itself heavily in debt to foreign investors. A sharp slowdown in the economy can lead to firms being unable to service their debts to the financial sector, which will in effect become a part owner of these firms. The financial sector itself, however, may not be able to service its debts and may shift hands to foreign investors.

This year, between January 1, 2020, and April 1, 2020, the rupee fell more than 8 percent against the dollar, sending tremors among corporate borrowers. In the wake of depreciation, Indian firms would have to shell out more rupees to service their foreign debt. If the rupee were to keep depreciating for a period of time, a certain percentage of firms would be unable to sustain this.

So rapid was the growth of such borrowings that, despite the RBI placing a limit of ECBs at 6.5 percent of GDP, the actual level of ECBs on December 31, 2019, appears to have long breached that limit, at 7.6 percent of GDP.

Shrinking the Micro, Small, and Medium Sectors

At the same time, the crisis of the last five years has had the effect of *shrinking* the micro, small, and medium enterprises (MSME) sector. While official estimates say MSMEs account for 45 percent of manufacturing output, 40 percent of total exports, and nearly 31 of GDP, the government has failed to conduct a census of the sector since

2006–07.[117] The last *sample* survey of such enterprises was for 2015–16, that is, before demonetization.[118] The government follows the untenable method of basing its estimates of informal sector growth on formal sector growth, thereby systematically concealing the scale of the crisis in the former sector, such as after demonetization.[119]

In stark contrast to the debt binge in the large enterprise sector, the MSME sector has been on a starvation diet. The already meagre bank credit to micro and small units has been falling further as a percentage of total bank credit, from 6.3 percent in February 2015 to 4.2 percent in February 2020. The corresponding figures for medium units are 2.2 and 1.2 percent (Chart 7). Bank credit to such units has even fallen *in absolute terms*, after discounting for inflation, as shown by chart 8. Thus, bank credit has fallen in real terms by 19 percent for micro and small units, and 33 percent for medium units.

Parasitic Extractions from MSMEs as Borrowers and Forced Lenders

Two striking facts are well-known in financial circles, but little mentioned in discussions about the economy. First, small and medium firms are sucked dry by different layers of the financial sector. According to an RBI committee, formal sector institutions—banks

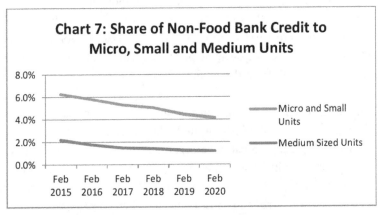

Source: Reserve Bank of India.

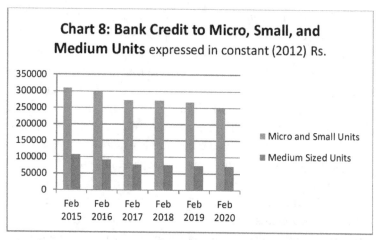

Source: Reserve Bank of India. Deflated by new consumer price index (rural and urban combined).

and non-banking financial corporations—account at best for only 40 percent of the credit needs of the MSME sector.[120] The gap, to the extent it is met, is met by the "informal sector"—moneylenders of one type or another. Interest rates for MSMEs on bank debt are much higher than for other industrial borrowers.[121] The All India MSME Association reports that interest rates for MSMEs are between 12 and 15 percent on bank credit, 18 percent on non-banking financial corporation loans, and 24 percent on loans from moneylenders.[122]

Second, as the RBI Committee puts it, large corporate firms that purchase goods or services from MSMEs "tend to use MSMEs as an alternative to banks" by delaying payments. This is a form of forcible interest-free credit from the small to the big.

> In order to delay payments, buyers have incentives to raise objections or point errors in submitted bills. . . . Like in many other markets, in India, most large corporates operate with MSMEs only on a credit basis. When the buyer does not honour the invoices on time, MSMEs face a financial crunch in the business. Their interest burden increases, cash flow becomes stressed and business continuity is impacted. Such MSMEs hesitate to file

complaint against large buyers to MSEFC or fight a legal battle with the buyer to enforce the contract.[123]

The committee estimates that the average number of debtor days (days until payment is received for work done) is consistently over ninety for the MSMEs. From the financial year 2016–17 there is a sharp increase and the figure for 2017–18 is over 210. How much credit is extorted in this fashion? According to the minister for MSMEs, Nitin Gadkari, dues to the MSME sector from the corporate sector and the government are over ₹5 trillion.[124] If this figure is correct, it appears that the overwhelming bulk of this would be from the private corporate sector.[125]

The Closing of Small and Medium Units

One telling indicator of the shrinkage of MSMEs is that employment in them has shrunk even as the employment of large and medium firms has slightly grown. According to surveys by the Centre for Monitoring the Indian Economy, total employment in the economy fell by four million (or 1 percent of total employment) just after the November 2016 demonetization; but the annual reports of large and medium sized companies showed a 2.6 percent increase in employment. This implies that the contraction was entirely in the informal sector.

Similarly, after the introduction of the goods and services tax, which imposed taxes and costs on small businesses that they were unable to bear, total employment shrank a further five million (between 2017 and 2018), whereas the larger companies, listed on the stock market, reported a 4.7 percent increase in employment. As Mahesh Vyas points out: "*This was expected* because the GST [goods and services tax] helped the larger and more [tax-]compliant companies take over the market shares vacated by the small enterprises. It is therefore quite likely that the brunt of the shocks of demonetisation and GST and the consequent economic slowdown thus far since 2017 has been borne by the unorganised [informal] sectors."[126]

The Small & Medium Business Development Chamber of India estimates that close to one million manufacturing units have closed since the end of 2016, due to demonetization, the goods and services tax, and lack of bank credit.[127]

It should be added that, in an underdeveloped country like India, where the informal sector makes up the overwhelming bulk of employment, survey data do not directly reveal the full extent of unemployment. Those working in the informal sector have no unemployment insurance to fall back on, and therefore keep working even if the income from such work is below subsistence levels. This is particularly true in the case of the self-employed. They are recorded as employed, but are, in any meaningful sense, unemployed to one extent or another. Since the informal sector is the source of the bulk of employment, the choking of this sector further aggravates the problem of inadequate aggregate demand.

Result of Debt Spree Followed by Stagnation and Decline: Major Restructuring of India's Economy in the Works

Thus, even before the COVID-19 crisis, the consequences of these developments were as follows:

1. The boom of 2003–08, or until 2010, was a credit boom fueled by a surge in capital inflows from abroad. In this boom phase, public assets, government subsidies, and natural resources were transferred on a gargantuan scale to private parties, many of them engaged in setting up public-private partnerships in infrastructure.
2. The credit boom collapsed, first in 2008–09 and then again from 2010 onward. Since that stimulus has ended, GDP growth has been heading downward (the grave problems in the government's measures of growth merely understate the extent of the fall in recent years).

   The collapse of the credit boom thus foregrounded once more the longstanding *underlying dearth of demand* in the Indian economy and its *utterly skewed income and wealth distribution*. These constraints could not be overcome without fundamental social change. In the absence of a fresh bubble, the only means by which the rulers could have revived growth within the existing framework was through government spending.

3. However, external pressure ensured that the government steadily reduced its spending as a proportion of GDP from 2010–11 onward, which in turn ensured that growth would slow down (Chart 9). (The demonetization of 2016 and the introduction of the goods and services tax thereafter also dealt blows to the informal sector, where the bulk of non-agricultural workers are employed, and thus further depressed demand and growth.)

Slowing growth also punched gaping holes in the government's tax revenues: the 2018–19 net tax revenues of the central government, which were budgeted at 7.9 percent of GDP, turned out to be just 6.9 percent, a shortfall of ₹1.6 trillion—what the director of the Finance Ministry-funded National Institute for Public Finance and Policy termed a "silent fiscal crisis."[128] The shortfall in tax revenues resulted in the central government's spending being cut by a further ₹1.2 trillion in 2018–19 in order to keep down the fiscal deficit. This spending cut further slowed the economy.

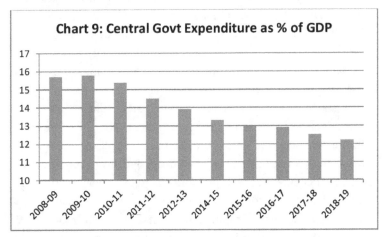

Source: *Economic Surveys* (New Delhi: Government of India, Ministry of Finance, Department of Economic Affairs, Economic Division).

4. During the period up to 2011, the corporate sector had borrowed from public sector banks and made investments on the basis of extravagant projections of growth. Once growth slowed and the government would not spend to revive it, large segments of the corporate sector were not earning enough to meet their interest obligations. The generous "restructuring" of their debt, including by surreptitiously providing them fresh loans to service their earlier ones, provided the promoters escape routes, but could not financially revive these projects.

5. In the period after 2010–11, the corporate sector also built up a heavy load of external commercial borrowings, rising from $70.7 billion in March 2010 to $223.8 billion in December 2019—that is, a growth of $153 billion, or ₹10.9 trillion at the then prevailing exchange rate. Not all of this was an additional debt (since some of it substituted debt to Indian banks) and some of this debt brought them temporary relief in the form of cheaper loans. But it created a ticking time bomb, since it was largely contracted on the dangerous assumption that the rupee to dollar exchange rate would remain stable. Any sharp fall in the rupee's value would send borrowing firms into a crisis.

6. The described situation implies that, in a situation of crisis, *both the government and the private sector would part with assets*, albeit for different reasons. The private sector would do so because it is the defined course under capitalism for a firm that cannot sustain its debt burden. The government would do so, using the *excuse* of reducing the fiscal deficit. However, that is not the *reason* it parts with assets. The reason the government parts with assets is simply that this is the defined course of development tied to foreign capital. In the neoliberal era, this course dictates that public sector assets must be privatized. Any defiance of foreign investors' directives (once articulated by the IMF/World Bank, but today increasingly by international credit rating agencies) would invite instant punishment in the form of capital outflow and crisis, but Indian rulers have no desire or intention to mount such defiance.

7. During a crisis, *assets are inevitably sold at distress prices* and the

only parties with the cash to buy them may be foreign firms and perhaps a handful of large Indian firms with special access to liquidity.
Reportedly, "three large Indian companies—HDFC Ltd, Reliance
[Industries Limited,] and Larsen and Toubro—managed to access
almost 39 per cent of all non-convertible debentures floated under
this facility in April. Six of the top 15 bond issues under this facility
were to large private corporations, accounting for 47.46 per cent of
all issues amounting to Rs.85,232 crore [₹852.32 billion]."[129]

8. As we saw, the pre-COVID-19 crisis had already brought about a
destruction of informal sector enterprises. Now, these enterprises
have been hit even more severely by the lockdown and the risk is
not confined to the micro and small units. What is crucial to grasp
is that this shift is not temporary: *many enterprises and livelihoods
will not return.* What we saw with demonetization and the goods
and services tax was merely the prelude. As V. Sridhar notes:

> In short, the writing is on the wall for smaller Indian
> companies.
> If this logic of letting the small perish is pursued to its logi-
> cal conclusion, it will have devastating consequences for the
> overall economy. . . . In fact, the contagion, if it takes effect,
> will not remain confined to small businesses, many medium
> and large companies may go bankrupt too. The government
> appears to be inclined to let the assets of these companies
> be liquidated by banks that will convert their loans into
> equity.[130]

We already have an economy in which the levels of employment are very low by world standards—using the Centre for
Monitoring the Indian Economy's definition, less than 40 percent
of the working-age population is employed.[131] These low employment levels are now set to fall further. This high-unemployment
economy will become the new "normal." Survey data of the Centre
for Monitoring the Indian Economy indicate that salaried jobs in
India plummeted from 86 million in March 2020 to just 65 million

in August, an astounding loss of *21 million jobs*. It is unclear how many of these jobs—considered better-than-casual labor or self-employment—will ever return.

Governments worldwide are contemplating schemes of universal basic income as a political method of disorienting the unemployed and preventing political unrest among them without providing employment, which is what they really need. The Indian government too is working out how to use such politically disorienting schemes while spending negligible sums on them. The COVID-19 crisis and its aftermath may offer them the scope to experiment in this field.

9. At the same time, in an effort to revive corporate appetite for investment amid a drought of demand, the state is carrying out aggressive changes ("reforms") to reduce wages, demolish the lingering remnants of workers' legal rights, make acquisition of peasant land easier, remove all restrictions on private capital in various sectors such as mining, further relax environmental regulations, and in general promise private capital greater "ease of doing business" (even making state governments' ability to borrow contingent on their fulfilling "ease of doing business" norms set by the center).

10. Taken together, *this is a comprehensive, multilayered restructuring of the Indian economy. Labor is being restructured in favor of capital, small firms are being restructured or destroyed in favor of big capital, the public sector is being cannibalized by private capital, and the domestic economy as a whole is being restructured in favor of foreign capital.*

While observers have to one extent or another noted the first three restructurings listed, the last has gone virtually without note. It is a historic turning point of great and devastating significance for the Indian people and the Indian nation.

THE RESTRUCTURING HAS ALREADY STARTED

The outlined trends were already being manifested before COVID-19.

Buying Opportunities in the Share Market

Foreign portfolio investors' holdings in the Indian share market are very large—they own over 40 percent of non-promoter holdings of the Nifty 500. Thus, taken as a bloc, they have an overwhelming impact on the share market. At a time of crisis, foreign portfolio investors tend to exit some of their holdings and the market as a whole declines. When this happens, the market value of foreign portfolio investors' holdings falls. However, like any canny investor, they use periods of downturn in the share market to buy shares at low prices.

The returns over the years have been huge. The *historical* value of FPI into Indian equities (that is, the sum of all the foreign capital inflows into the Indian share market) was $149 billion at the end of December 2019, but the *market* value of FPI holdings by then was above $463 billion—over three times more.[132] Thus, the recent fall in the Indian share market offered "buying opportunities" for foreign portfolio investors. There was huge net outflow of foreign portfolio capital in March, April, and May, but net flows turned positive once again in June. Further such opportunities may emerge in the coming months.

This helps understand why, even at the height of the lockdown, the Indian government deemed the share market an "essential service" and kept it running, even as foreign investors withdrew large sums. For foreign investors, absolute freedom of entry and exit is essential to maximizing gains, no matter how disruptive the impact on the host economy. The host economy in this case protected their power to disrupt. It is revealing that, at the same time, the government was denying Indian laborers the freedom to return to their villages and passenger trains were not considered an essential service. There could be no more stark or literal illustration of the neoliberal tenet of complete mobility of capital and immobility (even shackling) of labor.

A Silent Wave of Foreign Takeovers in the Private Corporate Sector

In research reports and the financial media, the debt crisis of the Indian corporate sector is presented quite frankly as a goldmine for foreign investors. The U.S.-based consulting firm McKinsey says: "The restructuring of stressed loans, which amounted to $146 billion on banks' books in December 2017, will create a one-time opportunity for investors with the risk appetite and operational turnaround expertise in several sectors needed to deploy capital at scale."[133]

In the last three years, there has been a surge in the number of "control deals" (when a firm changes hands) by foreign investors. In 2017–18, Indian investors accounted for 76 percent of control deals in India, but in 2018–19, the situation was reversed: foreign investors accounted for 79 percent of such deals.[134] The trend has continued in 2019–20.

Among such foreign investors are foreign firms as well as different types of investment funds, including private equity funds. Private equity funds raise capital from institutions or individuals and directly invest in private companies by negotiation with the promoters. They may buy either minority stakes, controlling stakes, or the entire share capital.

According to a November 2019 report commissioned by the Confederation of Indian Industry, foreign private equity firms invested $133.4 billion in Indian firms between January 2012 and August 2019, with the figure rising sharply in the last five years and the size of deals growing. Earlier, foreign private equity investors in India tended to be passive, but now deals in which private equity firms gain *control* of the target firm have risen to $9.9 billion in 2018. Private equity firms have now reportedly earmarked $100 billion to invest in Indian firms.[135]

In earlier years, the managements of larger Indian firms effectively resisted takeover bids. Hence, private equity firms targeted smaller or newer enterprises. R. Nagaraj notes:

Since such foreign funds, seeking managerial control by hostile takeover bids, were apparently frustrated in their efforts, they probably went after newer, and relatively smaller, enterprises and unlisted companies, when such investments were permitted.

Chart 10: Historical Private Equity Investments (US $ billion)

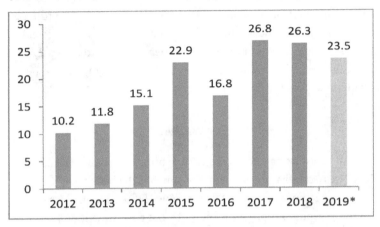

*Data for 2019 cover only eight months, from January to August. Source: Vikram Utamsingh, Nandini Chopra, Nikhil Shah, and Harkamal Ghuman, *India's M&A and Distressed Opportunity Landscape* (Mumbai: Alvarez & Marsal, 2019), based on Bain Private Equity Report 2019 and VCC Edge. Figures include venture capital investments.

Private equity capital, in particular, apparently discovered an opportunity in these investments, which could be termed "predatory lending". On the flip side, promoters of many Indian firms sought to leverage such foreign funds to leapfrog into the big league, overlooking the downside risks of high costs of external debt in terms of domestic currency (when market conditions turned adverse).[136]

The comment was prescient. In 2019, the promoter of Cafe Coffee Day committed suicide, leaving a note to the board that he was under pressure from a private equity firm, as well as lenders and tax authorities.

As the growth slowdown persists, an increasing number of large firms find it impossible to climb out of their debt traps. Fitch Ratings estimates stressed corporate debt in India at $260 billion and major groups such as the Jaypee Group, the Anil Dhirubhai Ambani Group,

Lanco and Essar faced insolvency.[137] As a result, a growing number of large Indian corporate firms have either had to sell important assets to foreign investors or surrendered control of their firms. According to a senior partner of the law firm AZB and partners, "given the stressed asset landscape, the number of control deals is likely to increase."[138]

We list here a few instances of asset sales, either completed or being negotiated, collected from media reports.

Distress Is All

Foreign investors have also taken over a number of road projects from debt-stressed Indian promoters. Presumably, the banks that lent large sums for such projects have taken sizable "haircuts," which may later require recapitalization of the banks by the government:

> In a new trend in the road infrastructure space in India, pension funds, sovereign wealth funds and private equity funds from Canada, Abu Dhabi, Australia and Singapore are seen emerging as new owners of road assets. . . .
>
> So far, these funds have collectively pumped in about ₹20,000–₹25,000 crore [₹200–250 billion] in up-and-running road assets and more funds are on their way. "Ownership of road assets has significantly changed over the last two years," said Jagannarayan Padmanabhan, director and practice leader, Transport Infrastructure Advisory, Crisil Risk & Infrastructure Solutions.
>
> "Earlier it was L&T IDPL, Ashoka Buildcon, IL&FS and others who were the road developers. Now, you are having a separate set of owners of assets who were not active in this space. These include GIC, CDPQ, CTPID, CPPIB, Macquarie and Esquire Capital, who have now become owners of road assets.". . .
>
> "What this means is that other than NHAI, foreign investors are controlling a certain percentage of India's road assets."[139]

A similar process is under way in solar energy and other renewables firms, which enjoy large subsidies and other forms of official

TABLE 5.1: Sale or Prospective Sale of Assets to Foreign investors by Debt-Stressed Indian Promoters

Indian Promoter	Asset	Foreign Purchaser (actual/prospective)	Comments
Max Group	Corporate hospital chain (13 hospitals)	PE major KKR-backed Radiant Life Sciences	
Max Group	Max Bupa health insurance	True North (PE firm)	
Anil Ambani	Mutual fund (43% stake)	Nippon Asset Management	Sold for Rs 65 billion
Anil Ambani	Home finance co.; majority stake	Talks with global investors	
S. & R. Ruia	Aegis BPO	Capital Square (PE firm)	Rs 44 billion
S. & R. Ruia	Equinox office complex, Mumbai	Brookfield (PE firm)	
Capt. Nair & family	Four marquee hotels	Brookfield (PE firm)	Rs 39.5 billion
B.M. Khaitan	Eveready Batteries	Talks on with Duracell, Energizer	
DHFL	Avanse financial services	Warburg Pincus PE	Several Indian bidders backed out for lack of funds
DHFL	Aadhar Housing financial services	Blackstone PE	
GMR infrastructure	49% stake in GMR airport business	Groupe ADP (France)	Sold for Rs 107.8 billion
GVK Group	Bengaluru airport; entire 43% stake	Fairfax PE	Helped bring down group debt significantly

Source: Media reports.

promotion. As international pressure builds for India to "green" its energy sector, these firms may enjoy rapid growth in the future. In 2019, the entire renewables sector had been "on the verge of implosion" due to debt.

That implosion did not come because of one key reason—the Indian renewables industry is now awash in foreign capital that has few other places to go. And the quest for safe havens may only heighten during a pandemic, turning India's renewable energy farms into a terrain for great games....

This influx of capital is already changing the ownership structure of Indian renewable energy assets, with foreign investors creating platforms that buy out portfolios belonging to different developers for long-term returns, or bringing in equity stake that turbocharge a developer's ability to bid for more greenfield projects. The largest home-grown developers from a few years ago have sold either controlling or significant equity stake to overseas investors.[140]

Among the prominent foreign investors in renewables are private equity firms such as the United States' KKR and Canada's Brookfield, as well as oil firms such as Total (France) and BP (United Kingdom). Three major deals for $400–500 million each have taken place in the first half of 2020. In the words of an investment banker, "in India, a rupee into renewables can give an investor a standard return on equity of 12–15%; that's 7–10% on the dollar, Jhawar says. "That's far above anything that global capital can earn in OECD [Organisation for Economic Co-operation and Development] countries."[141]

A *Bloomberg* report notes that foreign financial investors in India are not interested in new ventures. Rather, they are keen to buy Indian assets at depressed prices: "*distress is all that excites PE [private equity] investors now.*"[142] The greater the depression, the greater the distress, and the greater the scope for foreign investors to pick up assets at distress prices.

We need to see in this light the entire set of policies since 2010—the reduction in government spending and thereby reduction in aggregate demand, a monetary policy aimed at curbing demand, the Asset Quality Review classifying a large number of corporate debts as non-performing assets, the legislation of an Insolvency and Bankruptcy Code to speed up the process of putting these debts on the market, and

RBI circulars all aimed at further speeding up this process. The title of the recent research report commissioned by the Confederation of Indian Industry refers to India's "Distressed Opportunity Landscape." (This is a peculiar joining of words, since the distress is for one party while the opportunity is for another.) The report warns that any increase in funds available domestically would make the targeted firms more expensive for foreign investors to buy: "Despite the optimistic outlook of the India PE [private equity] market, investors have some concerns going forward, including: High asset pricing driven by increase in capital availability."[143]

Importantly, especially after the collapse of the giant private lender IL&FS in September 2018, the entire non-banking financial corporation sector found it difficult to borrow money. As mentioned earlier, a large number of such non-banking financial corporations borrowed abroad in the last two years. However, many firms to which the non-banking financial corporations lent may find themselves in dire straits as the economy goes deeper into depression in the coming period. If the debtor firms' default, the non-banking financial corporations may come to control them. At the same time, the non-banking financial corporations themselves may be unable to service their debt to foreign lenders. In such a situation, foreign lenders may come to effectively control sizable assets of non-financial firms.

The Rescue of Specific Business Groups

It is necessary to note that specific large domestic business groups considered close to the ruling party, though very heavily indebted, have been saved the rigors of the Insolvency and Bankruptcy Code process with the help of special deals. M. Rajshekhar describes one such remarkable instance.[144] The Essar Group was one of India's largest stressed debtors and its prize asset, Essar Oil Ltd, seemed set to be sold at distress prices. Then, in 2015, India's public sector oil exploration firm, Oil and Natural Gas Corporation, decided to purchase a share in an oilfield owned by the Russian firm Rosneft at a much higher-than-expected price. In turn, Rosneft bought Essar Oil, the refining business of the Essar Group, at a much higher-than-expected price. Analysts at Kotak Institutional Equities said in a note to clients that "the formal announcement of the deal at the recent BRICS summit in the presence of the political leaders of India and Russia suggests a high degree of involvement of the Indian government in the transaction. We note that Indian PSU oil companies had earlier purchased a 49.9% stake in the Vankor oil block of Rosneft."[145] Rajshekhar notes: "By the end, not only had Rosneft accessed the India market, its losses from overpayment were offset by the $6 billion it made from the sale of its oilfields…to Indian public sector companies. As for Essar, which had been struggling to make interest payments on loans, it made a packet instead of losing its refinery to bankruptcy proceedings. A part of this adventure, however, was capitalised by Indian oilcos."[146]

There are other instances of select top business groups being snatched from the jaws of bankruptcy in this fashion. For instance, the Gujarat government carved out a rescue for thermal power plants owned by the leading business houses Tata and Adani and Essar, while the bankrupt Anil Ambani group was mysteriously selected by the French firm Dassault as its local partner for manufacturing Rafale fighter jets for the Indian air force. Nevertheless, these exceptions do not contradict the fact that the Insolvency and Bankruptcy Code process generates a continuing, rich stream of bad debt assets to be sold at distress prices to those with cash.

Implications of Foreign Takeovers

In the boom phase, as we discussed, the Indian private corporate sector's public-private partnership projects received a range of bounties from the government—subsidies, tax concessions, cheap land, free or undervalued government-owned infrastructure, and so on. The public sector banks provided loans for these projects. Thus, the projects themselves were a form of alienating public assets.

However, now that the Indian private promoters have defaulted on the loans, many of these projects are being transferred to foreign investors and the banks are accepting large "haircuts" (as much as 85 percent) on the sums due to them. This amounts to a large transfer of India's public wealth to foreign investors, on distress terms—a *second alienation*, as it were.

Let us take a hypothetical example. A private investor puts up an infrastructure project but inflates the cost by 80 percent. Under pressure from the government, a public sector bank extends a loan for two-thirds of the stated project cost and the private investor puts in one-third. This is celebrated as rapid growth of investment by the private corporate sector. However, in fact, the bank has funded 120 percent of the actual cost of the project and the private investor has already made money by getting kickbacks from suppliers of equipment and materials.

The investor then defaults on the loan and, after many years of unsuccessful restructuring and additional financing, the project goes before the National Company Law Tribunal. In a depressed environment, the only bid comes from a foreign investor, who offers much less than the actual cost of the project. (Reportedly, buyers of insolvent thermal power projects are paying no more than ₹25 million to ₹30 million per megawatt, whereas a new thermal power plant costs around ₹50 million per megawatt to set up.[147]) The public sector bank has no option but to take a massive "haircut" and accept the offer. This is then celebrated as India's success in attracting foreign investment.

Further, as foreign investors own an increasingly larger share of the Indian corporate sector, the drain from India will increase. One has only to look at the drain from India on account of just one foreign-owned company, Maruti Suzuki, to get a sense of this.[148]

Finally, the growing weight of foreign-owned firms in the Indian corporate sector will further shape government policy in favor of foreign investors. In the (admittedly unlikely) event that any future government were to attempt to regulate them in the public interest, foreign firms could twist the government's arm with the influence of their home countries or by applying for the dispute to be settled by international arbitration abroad, which is heavily tilted in favor of foreign investors.

We should take note of an additional route by which foreign

investors may reap the benefits of India's corporate debt crisis and predatory acquisitions. In this two-step operation, a powerful Indian business house acquires a debt-stressed firm at a depressed price. It then sells stakes in its own—now expanded—firm to foreign investors. Thus, Reliance Industries' retail venture, India's largest corporate retail enterprise, announced in August 2020 that it would acquire the second-largest retail firm for $3.3 billion. In September 2020, two U.S.-based investment firms, Silver Lake and KKR, announced investments in Reliance Retail totaling $1.7 billion. According to a *Bloomberg* report, as yet not officially confirmed, Reliance has offered Amazon a 40 percent stake in Reliance Retail for $20 billion.[149] Similarly, Gautam Adani, another corporate chieftain closely identified with the ruling party, has recently acquired control of the Mumbai airport at a depressed price from the debt-stressed GVK group.[150] Since the Adani group itself has large debts, it may at some point invite foreign investors to take stakes in its frenetically expanding airport business.

Privatization

The U.S.-based consultancy Boston Consulting Group, now a key advisor to the Indian government on the COVID-19 crisis, spelled out in 2018 what it called "the $75 Trillion Opportunity in Public Assets":

> Governments around the world are under enormous financial pressure. Budgets remain constrained in many countries while the need for investment—particularly in infrastructure—is growing.
>
> A solution, however, is hiding in plain sight. Central governments worldwide control roughly $75 trillion in assets, according to conservative estimates—a staggering sum equal to the combined GDP of all countries. . . .
>
> Government leaders must take aggressive action to harness the value of the public assets under their control. . . .
>
> Governments should consider three main transaction models:

- Corporatization
- Partnerships.
- Privatization.[151]

A major, even central, gain for foreign investors from the regime of fiscal austerity is that it invariably includes a program of privatization. The pressure to reduce the fiscal deficit is, as it were, the lever. The prize is public assets.

As such, even within the framework of orthodox economics, there is no justification for linking privatization to an attempt to bridge the fiscal deficit (that is, the gap between spending and revenues, which is made up by borrowing). After all, privatization is the sale of government assets, but the fiscal deficit is largely made up of current (recurring) expenditures, which create no assets. Selling assets to pay for running expenses is a recipe for a deeper mess. Hence, privatization must be dressed up as "reducing the burden of the public sector on government finances," "increasing efficiency," "increasing national wealth," and other such euphemisms. We can easily judge the worth of this argument by noting that, in practice, the government has never used the proceeds of privatization to invest in other long-lasting, efficiency-improving assets. It merely credits the proceeds of privatization to its "non-tax revenues"—that is, it uses it to meet its running expenses.

The "Prime Minister's Economic Package in the Fight Against COVID-19," as presented by the finance minister over five days, remarkably contained virtually nothing related to public health. Rather, the centerpiece was privatization—of the coal sector, the mineral sector, airports, electricity distribution, the defense industry, atomic energy, "social infrastructure" (related to education, health care, water supply, sanitation, and so on), and the space program. Whether or not private investments in all these fields materialize, one point was categorically stated: virtually all public sector enterprises, barring a handful, are to be sold off.

The Government of India ("GOI") introduced a slew of reforms from May 13th to May 17th 2020. . . .

Part 5 of the Reforms clearly stated that the GOI would soon announce a policy whereby

- List of strategic sectors requiring presence of Public Sector Enterprises (PSEs) in public interest will be notified
- In strategic sectors, **at least one enterprise will remain in the public sector but private sector will also be allowed**
- In other sectors, **PSEs will be privatized** (timing to be based on feasibility etc.)
- To minimise wasteful administrative costs, **number of enterprises in strategic sectors will ordinarily be only one to four; others will be privatised/ merged/ brought under holding companies**[152]

The list of "strategic sectors" has not yet been spelled out, but it is thought to contain atomic energy and defense and the space program. Other possibilities include oil and gas, telecom, and banking and financial services.

The scale of the proposed sell-off is staggering. The *Economic Survey 2019–20* says there are about 264 central public sector enterprises under thirty-eight different ministries and departments. Of these, thirteen ministries and departments have around 10 central public sector enterprises each under its jurisdiction. Now, even in "strategic" sectors, the maximum is to be 4. For the remaining sectors, all firms are to be sold over time. Note that this agenda was in fact underway well before COVID-19 and the prime minister's "economic package"—the pandemic merely offered an excuse for advancing it even more aggressively.

The *Economic Survey* provides a one-point rationale for privatization, namely, that private firms are more profitable than public sector ones and that this "creates wealth." The author does not even once ask: For whom? Once a firm is private, it creates wealth for its private owners.

Thus, the chapter on privatization begins with the following strange argument: the government announced in November 2019 that the oil-refining and marketing giant Bharat Petroleum Corporation Limited

Chart 11: Profitable and Unprofitable Central Public Sector Enterprises under Various Ministries

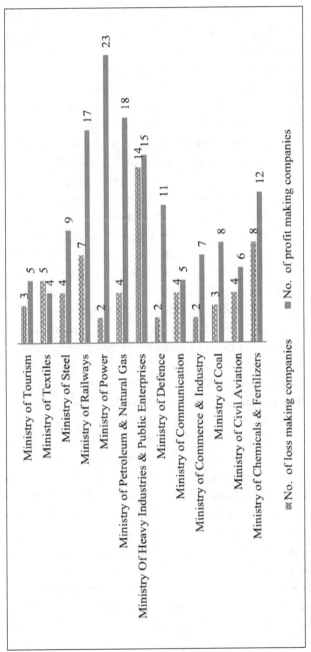

Source: *Economic Survey 2019–20* (New Delhi: Government of India, Ministry of Finance, Department of Economic Affairs, Economic Division, 2020).

(BPCL) would be privatized—that is, the remaining 53 percent shares
owned by the government would be sold. At this point, the share price
of BPCL rose, whereas that of the similar public sector firm Hindustan
Petroleum Corporation Limited (HPCL) did not. This increase trans-
lates into "an increase in the value of shareholders' equity of BPCL by
around ₹33,000 crore [₹330 billion]…and thereby a *rise in national
wealth* by the same amount."[153] This is a bizarre identification of a speculative rise in asset prices with an increase in national wealth.

BPCL has always been making profits, around ₹70–80 billion a
year for the past five years (indeed, almost all privatizations are of
profit-making companies). The rise in the share price of BPCL after
the government's announcement of its plans to sell its remaining 53
percent of shares merely indicated that share market investors anticipated that, once privatized, the firm would be able to increase its
profits further by jacking up petroleum product prices.

The logic is simple. India has nearly 260 million metric tons of refining capacity, of which at present 80 are in the private sector and nearly
180 in the public sector. With the privatization of BPCL, roughly 110
metric tons of refining capacity would be in the private sector, and
150 in the public sector—closer to an even match. If HPCL is later
privatized too, as the government indicates, the two would be evenly
matched, with a lone Indian Oil Corporation left in the public sector.
Furthermore, 75 percent of petroleum products distribution is in the
public sector and 25 percent in the private sector. With the privatization of BPCL, this would shift to 50 percent in each.

In such a changed situation, it would no longer be possible for the
government to dictate petroleum product prices, even if it wanted.
Indeed, "bidders [for BPCL] will need assurance that the regime of
free-market pricing for fuel stays. Last year, investors in state-owned
oil firms got a shock when they were reportedly asked to sacrifice on
marketing margins to help lower the cost of fuel in retail markets."[154]
A private owner of BPCL might also shut unprofitable retail outlets,
depots, and terminals. It might not participate in special government
schemes to extend cooking gas to backward rural areas, just as private
banks do not bother to set up branches there.

Thus, it is not increased efficiency, nor consequent "wealth creation," that share market investors anticipated when they were bidding up share prices of BPCL. They simply anticipated increased extractions from the public in a private sector-dominated oil pricing regime.

BPCL: Privatizing During a Depression

However, the *Economic Survey*'s triumphant glee at the rise in BPCL share prices up to January 14, 2020, has come up against an embarrassing development: the share price has dropped sharply since then. On August 19, 2020, BPCL's share price is 14.5 percent lower than on January 14. It is even slightly lower than on September 13, 2019 (when the first report of BPCL's possible privatization appeared in the media). That is, by the *Survey*'s own method, the "increase in national wealth" claimed by the *Survey* has evaporated. Such is the quicksilver nature of "national wealth" in the imaginings of the government's top economic officials.

In these depressed conditions, it is clear that the government is getting very low offers from bidders. Thus, the government has had to extend the deadline three times (from May 2 to June 13 to July 31 to September 30) for bids showing interest in buying a stake. However, the minister for petroleum and natural gas, Dharmendra Pradhan, recently stated in an interview: "Let me categorically assure investors and stakeholders, recently the Finance minister on her package announcement has categorically come out with a new policy approach on PSUs. For BPCL we have taken a decision prior to COVID-19 situation and we are very firm on our decision."[155]

If the government proceeds with privatization despite the depressed economic environment, as the minister promises to do, the price obtained for BPCL will be correspondingly low.

How is BPCL to be valued for the purpose of privatization? We do not know how the government plans to do this. There are a number of methods used in valuing an asset for the purpose of sale, but only two are relevant here. First, how much interest would the government have to pay if it instead borrowed the sum (that it would get as the sale price), compared to the stream of revenues it would lose after privatization (53 percent of the future profits of BPCL)?

It is difficult to know what the future stream of profits of a company would be, since the projection is only as good as the assumptions on which it is based. However, we do know the other relevant fact: that the central government can borrow at a low rate of interest, at present just 6 percent a year. Hence, any future stream of revenues on BPCL that is higher than, say, 6 percent per year of the proposed sale price, would make it unprofitable for the government to privatize.

A second method is to look at the replacement value of BPCL: What would it cost the government today to put up the assets that BPCL owns? According to the Public Sector Officers' Association, the present worth of BPCL's physical assets is ₹7.5 trillion, which would mean that the government's stake is worth at least ₹4 trillion, even without adding a premium for handing over control of the company. Analysts at ICICI Securities provide a much lower figure of the value of BPCL's assets, at ₹946 per share, which they claim is based on the value of recent transactions and, in the case of the replacement cost of the refineries, based on HPCL's upcoming Rajasthan refinery.[156] At this price, BPCL's assets would be worth around ₹2.05 trillion. But even at this lower price, the government shareholding, at 53 percent, would be worth ₹1.09 trillion. This is about ₹350 billion higher than the higher figures being discussed in the media for the sale of the government stake.

Nor could it be otherwise. These privatizations are distress sales and the number of potential purchasers usually number just four or five. Nevertheless, as tax revenues are certain to collapse this year, the government will be under pressure to try to sell assets in an attempt to keep the fiscal deficit down. Moody's has now downgraded India, citing, among other things, the deteriorating fiscal position of the government and its weak implementation of "reforms." A key "reform" desired by the credit rating agencies is privatization.

It is true that foreign investors are not the only possible beneficiaries of the sale of BPCL. Along with a few multinationals, Reliance Industries Limited, the largest Indian private firm in the petroleum sector, is a likely bidder. However, this merely validates our contention that the privatization program as a whole is a bonanza for foreign investors and a handful of top Indian firms with access to funds. (Foreign investors stand to gain *through* the highly profitable Reliance Industries Limited as well. Foreign portfolio investors hold half of the non-promoter holding in the firm. Moreover, as part of a strategy to pare down its large debt burden, Reliance Industries Limited has been selling stakes in its different ventures to foreign investors and is in negotiations to sell stakes in its oil business too.[157])

We have taken BPCL merely as an example. The fact is that privatization is almost always carried out at depressed prices. This is true worldwide as well as in India. Thus, the Committee on Disinvestment of Shares in Public Sector Enterprises, headed by then-RBI governor C. Rangarajan, admitted in 1993 that "there has been virtually universal criticism of underpricing of shares wherever disinvestment has taken place." Nevertheless, the committee recommended massive disinvestment.

Here, we have not gone into the basic arguments against privatization—namely, that under the existing economic system the public sector is meant to do what "market forces" (the private sector) have failed to do. Hence, privatization amounts to an attack on the established social claims of the people in favor of large capital. The argument here is limited to showing the extent of bounty received by foreign capital and a few native large capitalists.

* * *

Some Distinct Features

As can be seen from the examples of other countries in the endnote, India's experience is not unique. However, three differences are worth noting.

First, in the case of those countries, the IMF (and the EU and the

European Central Bank in the case of Greece) played the leading role on behalf of international capital. In India's case, the IMF is relatively in the background and the lead role is played by credit rating agencies such as Moody's, Standard and Poor, and Fitch Ratings. Thus, while the IMF's direct intervention was visible to the people of the affected country, in the case of India, foreign capital's intervention appears in the garb of impersonal market forces.

Second, India is not yet under the same level of pressure as the countries discussed in the endnote. For the moment, there is no foreign exchange crisis and indeed capital inflows have revived, swelling the foreign exchange reserves. The government no doubt is keenly aware of the underlying vulnerability of those reserves, but it is by no means implementing these measures at financial gunpoint, as it were.

Third, in the case of the Asian economies in 1997 and 1998, and Greece after 2010, public opposition and resistance manifested themselves strongly. The rulers of those countries therefore made noises of complaint, or at times refused to sign on the dotted line of the deals imposed by the foreign lenders. Of course, they finally abandoned their posture of resistance and became the instruments of the IMF/EU program.

However, in India, the rulers themselves have aggressively come forward with the package of austerity and "reforms" as their *own*. Even more outlandishly, they have promoted it as "self-reliance."

What the Rulers Bank On

The refusal of the rulers to spend and the aggressive "reforms" they are now embarking on may kindle unrest and resistance by sections of the people. What then gives them the confidence to proceed on their present course?

Evidently, they have assured themselves that their physical force and ideological hegemony over working people are sufficient to sail through the crisis. In this, the recently exacerbated communal divisions, which always existed but have taken particularly disturbing forms in the last six years, play an important role.

The rulers do not require the support of a majority of the people to exercise effective control; it is sufficient that they have the support of a sizable, vocal, and assertive social bloc. When properly mobilized, for example through demonstrations of support such as *thali* beating, conch blowing, and lamp lighting, this bloc can convey a sense of overwhelming strength and instill fear in weak and disorganized opponents of their policies. The prevailing atmosphere of panic and isolation can set the stage for more ominous political changes. The rulers have tested the waters over the past few months and they foresee no real obstacles to their plans.

However, in a situation of great upheaval and misery, the rulers' confidence may be ill judged. Conscious sections may emerge as an organized opposition to the current drive of the government. Starting precisely from the experience of the COVID-19 crisis, they may demand a rollback of privatization, the nationalization of different services to address people's needs, and the provision of a range of basic needs. If these spark a broader response among the people, developments may take a very different turn.

ENDNOTE: FINANCIAL CRISIS AS OPPORTUNITY FOR FOREIGN INVESTORS

During 1997 and 1998, a number of countries in southeast and east Asia suffered a crisis. The crisis began in May 1997 with a slide in the value of the Thai currency, the *baht*. It thereafter spread to Malaysia, the Philippines, Indonesia, Hong Kong, and South Korea, with foreign capital exiting and local currencies getting hammered. Even though these countries had very different economies, they had all carried out liberalization of external capital flows to one extent or another in recent years. Several of these countries now approached the IMF for emergency loans, which were given on very stiff conditions, requiring sweeping internal changes and causing massive unemployment, steep food price increases, and foreign takeovers. In the course of 1997 and 1998, the terms of these loans resulted in social unrest and political upheaval in these countries, including the fall of the thirty-one-year

Suharto regime in Indonesia in the face of mass protests. The lasting image of the period was a photograph of then-managing director of the IMF, Michel Camdessus, standing imperiously with folded arms over Suharto, who, head bowed, signed away his country's sovereignty in exchange for IMF funds. By December 1998, official studies estimated that 40 percent of Indonesia's population had fallen below the country's poverty line since the start of the crisis.

In fact, the IMF, under the tight control of the U.S. Department of the Treasury, used the crisis to engineer a foreign invasion of the economies of these countries. Thus, a calamity for the people of these countries turned out to be a useful episode for international capital, particularly U.S. capital.

South Korea

In June 1996, more than a year before the crisis hit South Korea, the U.S. Department of the Treasury spelled out its aims in an internal memo: opening up Korean debt and share markets further to foreign investors. This process had already been underway for some years and Korean corporate conglomerates (the *chaebol*) massively expanded their foreign borrowing, with debt to foreign banks tripling between 1994 and 1996, reaching $120 billion by late 1997.

This set Korea up for a fall. Once the crisis broke in Thailand, private capital inflows to Korea plummeted a staggering 8 percent of GDP. The exchange rate of the Korean currency, the won, halved (from ₩987 to $1 in November 1997 to ₩1900 to $1 in January 1998).[158]

Korea approached the IMF for a loan in December 1997, and the IMF set its terms: free capital markets from government control; the breakup of Korea's distinctive corporate conglomerates; the destruction of unions by bringing in labor market "flexibility"; making the central bank independent of democratic processes; an end to government intervention in external trade; and allowing the free entry of foreign investment, including hostile takeovers of Korean firms.

Before the crisis, South Korea, far from running a fiscal deficit, was in fact running a fiscal surplus—the same was true of Thailand,

Malaysia, and Indonesia. Even so, all these economies were told by the IMF to cut government spending in order to restore "confidence" in their currencies.[159] The IMF tightened the screws on Korean firms by jacking up interest rates to unbearable levels and closing down many banks. Aggregate demand plummeted. This was the *planned* outcome of the IMF measures:

> the IMF knew full well that the macro policies it imposed on Korea starting in December 1997 would lead to an economic collapse in 1998; an examination of newspaper and business press reports at that time demonstrate that everyone knew this. An economic collapse was the sine qua non [essential condition] of the US-IMF strategy. If the neoliberal powers had tried to impose their free-market revolution under normal conditions… they would have met strong political resistance from labor, large segments of the Korean people, and even some sectors of the business community.[160]

In the words of Larry Summers, deputy secretary of the U.S. Department of the Treasury at the time of the crisis, "times of financial emergency are times when [outside political] leverage is greatest." *The Wall Street Journal* and *New York Times* observed that the U.S. Department of the Treasury "calls the main shots at the IMF" and that "the IMF had succeeded in using its bailouts to force [Asian] nations to open their markets." The IMF acknowledged pressure from "the IMF's major shareholder governments. . . . The U.S. authorities in particular insisted that strong reforms should be a condition of IMF support." Then-managing director of the IMF Michel Camdessus unabashedly stated that "the Asian crisis was a 'blessing in disguise' because it gave the IMF the leverage to force structural policy changes *that the national governments would not otherwise accept.*"[161]

As part of the conditions for the IMF loan, South Korea abolished limits on the percentage of corporate stock that foreigners could own and eased foreign investment regulations in capital markets. The government permitted hostile mergers and acquisitions by foreign investors after 1998 and tried to sell financial institutions to foreign-ers. From 2001 onward, a second phase began, with further openings to FDI and incentives to foreign investors.[162] This set off a massive transfer of assets from Korean to foreign hands:

> Korean enterprises could meet the government demand to cut down their debts only through the extensive sale of real assets to foreigners. This forced Korean assets to be offered in a kind of fire sale, to which the collapse of the *won* also contributed.... Foreigners have gained strong influence over major Korean industries, including semiconductors, automobiles, electronics, telecommunications, petrochemicals, and finance. In mid-2001, foreigners owned 56 percent of the listed shares in Samsung Electronics, 63 percent of POSCO, and 57 percent of the listed stock of Hyundai Motors. . . .
>
> Many financial institutions were first sold to foreign private equity funds. . . . The share of foreign ownership of the eight large commercial banks rose from 12 percent in 1998 to 39 per-cent in 2003 and 64 percent in 2004. Foreigners now own more than half the shares of seven of the eight large banks, totally dominating commercial banking.[163]

The stock market too was taken over: the percentage of Korean stock market capitalization owned by foreigners rose from 14.6 per-cent in late 1997 to 36.6 in late 2001, to 42 percent in late 2004.[164] FPI and FDI together made up a staggering $62 billion between 1998 and 2000, but FPI does not add to productive capital and the over-whelming majority of FDI went to foreign acquisitions of domestic firms rather than new ("greenfield") investment.[165] After the reforms, investment slowed; lending by now-foreign-owned banks shifted from productive activities to consumer lending and away from small- and medium-sized firms; and the distribution of income became more unequal.[166] Restrictions on foreign ownership of land and real estate too were abolished in July 1998.

As part of the IMF conditions, the government embarked on

public sector retrenchments and privatization. Of the 108 state-owned enterprises, 38 were to be immediately privatized, 34 were to be gradually privatized, 9 would be merged into others or liquidated, and 21 would go through restructuring. In the course of this, eighty thousand people were to lose their jobs. The revenues of privatization were supposed to fund the government as it took over the debts of private banks. But no matter how much they sold, privatization never came close to generating the revenues needed and, instead, public debt surged.[167]

Another key demand of the IMF was "labor market flexibility." The Korean government promised the IMF that it would amend laws to ease layoffs and give freedom to private job placement and manpower leasing services. Workers with job security could thus be replaced with "contingent workers," or what are referred to elsewhere as "informal" workers without job security and statutory benefits.[168] In January 1998, the new president held a joint meeting with union leaders and big business, and got union leaders to agree to "flexibility." Unemployment soared as more than one hundred thousand workers were laid off every month of 1998 and the rank and file of the leading trade union revolted and forced the leaders to resign. They replaced them with contingent workers, minimizing labor costs—after such restructuring, "most estimates of the proportion of contingent workers range from 36% to 57%."[169]

In brief, South Korea underwent a program of restructuring on four fronts: from labor to capital, from small firms to big firms, from the public sector to the private corporate sector, and from domestic capital to international capital.

The sale of assets, whether private or public, to foreigners was done under distress conditions, further accentuated by a collapse in the Korean currency (which made Korean assets cheaper for foreigners). It yielded a bonanza for foreign capital, at great cost to the Korean people. Note that this financial invasion was carried out not on a hostile power, but on a country that had close military and strategic ties to the United States—and that had allowed thirty-six thousand U.S. troops to be stationed on its territory.

Thailand

Thailand underwent a similar restructuring under IMF dictates. Here, we would like to focus on the corporate restructuring that took place.

A study of Thailand's corporate sector in the wake of the crisis found that 26 percent of corporations were forced to change their ownership patterns during the crisis period, with forty-one firms changing to foreign ownership.[170] Nearly all major business groups had grown with the use of foreign loans in the period leading up to the crisis, and hence were vulnerable once the Thai currency value plunged. However, once the crisis set in, the business groups that tried to retain control of their empires collapsed. Whereas the ones that did not try to do so, but quickly sold assets to foreign firms and adapted themselves as their junior partners, recovered and prospered. Thus, the Thai Petrochemical Industry Group finally had to file for bankruptcy, whereas

> Siam Cement Group. . . . CP Group, the Thai Farmers Bank Group, the Bank of Ayudhya Group, the SPI Group, and the Central Department Store Group, launched reforms to downsize their widely diversified business activities…and promoted alliances with new foreign partners. The development of CP Group serves as a typical example.
>
> Immediately after the currency crisis, CP Group undertook drastic corporate restructuring and downsized its business by concentrating resources in two core fields: agro-industry and telecommunications. In the process, it transferred profitable sectors of its retail business to foreign partners and then deinvested from the petrochemical industry. . . .
>
> Through this reorganization, CPF became a holding company to supervise its operations in the agro-industry sector and the core firm to attract foreign investors. Owing to this corporate restructuring, CPF successfully attracted foreign investors, who took about 39% of total shareholdings, and quickly improved its financial indicators.[171]

Similarly, most of the financial sector came under foreign control.

The Invasion of Greece

Greece is not a third world country—nor is it an "emerging market economy," to use the current terminology. It is a member of three elite clubs: the club of advanced economies, the Organisation for Economic Co-operation and Development; the European Union; and the North Atlantic Treaty Organisation. Its merchant navy is the largest in the world. For a long time, it was one of the world's fastest-growing economies, and in 2008 its per capita income was over $32,000. In the period before the Great Financial Crisis of 2007–09, it experienced rapid growth, fueled by government deficits and foreign borrowings. Government debt was 109 percent of GDP at current market prices in 2008, a high figure, but comparable to figures for Belgium, Italy, and the United States, and much below the figure for Japan. With the Great Financial Crisis, growth of its two key industries, tourism and shipping, slowed and GDP fell by 1.8 percent in 2009. Nevertheless, until January 2010, Greece was still able to borrow internationally at reasonable rates.

However, in early 2010, allegations suddenly emerged that Greece was deliberately and illegally understating the size of its public debt. The eventual fresh audit performed under the supervision of European authorities could not find proof of illegality and revised the size of the debt upward by about 10 to 15 percent, not an earth-shaking sum. Nevertheless, the credibility of Greece's statistics had been destroyed by the media campaign.[172] In August 2010, an IMF officer was installed as the head of Greece's *official* statistical agency. He reported to the European Commission without reference to the board of the agency, revising government deficit and debt figures upward. (Eventually, he was found guilty of violations by Greek courts, but by then he had already left the country and now resides in the United States.) The European Commission seized the opportunity and accused Greece of statistical fraud. In these conditions, a market panic was created, the interest rates on Greek debt soared, effectively making it impossible for Greece to borrow on the international market.

The Course Not Taken

In 2009, about 80 percent of public debt was owed to external creditors. A large part of the public debt (€150 billion at the end of 2009) was held by foreign banks, mostly European.[173] At this point, Greece could have taken the course taken by Argentina earlier—namely, to default. In Argentina's case, the private foreign lenders were later forced to accept a large "haircut," that is, a reduction in debts, allowing the Argentinian economy to recover. The justification is clear: the lenders themselves bore a responsibility for extending loans that were beyond the capacity of the Greek economy to sustain. In addition to defaulting on private debt, Greece had the option of leaving the euro and returning to its own pre-2001 currency, which would give it flexibility in its exchange rate. While these steps may have inflicted a harsh immediate cost ("bitter medicine") on the Greek economy, they could have opened up a path to eventual recovery. The course the Greek ruling classes took made Greece swallow not the medicine, but the poison.

The "the first priority of the 'troika' has been to protect the lenders from losses and the Eurozone from the threat of a major rupture, as the IMF has openly admitted. . . . Greece had to be prevented from defaulting and exiting the EMU [Economic and Monetary Union of the European Union], while submitting to a programme along the lines of the Washington Consensus."[174] To preempt any independent course, the IMF and EU arranged a €73 billion bailout package for Greece. In fact, the bailout package served to pay back the European private banks that had lent Greece money. In this fashion, Greece's creditors shifted from private banks to public institutions, which made default much more difficult in international law.

A sovereign state could always default, assuming that the country would be prepared to shoulder the cost of legal proceedings and its exclusion from the financial markets for a period. . . .

In the case of Greece there is undeniable evidence that the IMF was fully aware of the importance of devaluation and

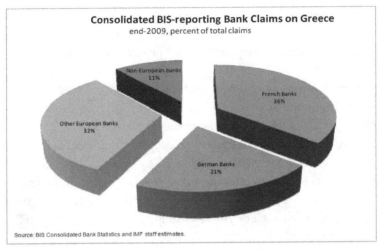

Source: International Monetary Fund, 2010.

debt restructuring already in 2010. However, EMU member-
ship made formal devaluation impossible and debt relief was
bluntly rejected by Eurozone lenders. Thus, the IMF laid great
stress on "internal devaluation" pivoting essentially on wage
reductions. . . . By its own admission, the IMF ignored its own
research and simply kowtowed to political pressure from the
lenders to Greece, who were among its major shareholders. In
2010, a Greek default, or even major debt restructuring, and
Greek exit from the EMU would have posed grave risks for
the banks of the lenders but also for the very survival of the
monetary union. From the perspective of the lenders, Greece
had to be kept in the EMU. It also had to bear the brunt of
the adjustment without debt restructuring or devaluation. The
EMU had placed the country in an iron cage and the results
would soon show.[175]

The IMF, the European Commission, and the European Central
Bank, collectively known as the *troika*, presided over all three "bailouts" until 2018. The price was a harsh austerity program for Greece
under the supervision of the troika: cuts in government expenditure,

large scale retrenchments, increases in taxes on consumption, and privatization.

To put it more simply, the troika's program meant that Greece would service its debt in the following ways: (1) by steeply reducing wages, so that people consumed less output; (2) turning over that "saved" output to foreign lenders; and (3) handing over Greece's precious assets to foreign lenders at depressed prices.

Through these measures, an unprecedented 11 percent of GDP was to be squeezed out from the Greek people to service loans. Of this, 9.2 percent was to be extracted *immediately*, a process known as "frontloading" (according to the IMF, "strong frontloading is expected to minimize implementation risk, avoid adjustment fatigue, and rebuild confidence swiftly"). The IMF stated:

> Expenditure measures are estimated at 5.2 percent of GDP. The elimination of the Easter, summer, and Christmas pensions and wages, as well as cuts in allowances and high pensions are frontloaded and will, by themselves, yield 2 percent of GDP of the 11 percent total package. Other expenditure cuts involve employment reductions, cuts in discretionary and low priority investment spending, untargeted social transfers, consolidation of local governments, and lower subsidies to public enterprises.
>
> Revenue measures add another 4 percent of GDP to the package. This includes an increase in the standard VAT rate from 21 to 23 percent and the reduced rate from 10 to 11 percent, moving lower taxed products such as utilities, restaurants and hotels to the standard VAT rate, and increasing excises on fuel, cigarettes, and tobacco to bring them in line with EU averages. Those measures yield 2.1 percent of GDP.[176]

The result was a catastrophic decline in Greece's economy. Demand collapsed. GDP declined by 25 percent between 2009 and 2016, and even in 2019 was 21 percent lower than a decade earlier.

Meanwhile, the public debt increased by about 10 percent, from €301 billion to €331 billion between 2009 and 2019 (see chart).

However, the burden of the debt is not reflected simply in the absolute figure of debt. A debt of ₹100,000 may be sustainable for a farmer who can sell their crop at a good price, but it becomes an unbearable burden if crop prices crash. What matters is thus the debt as a ratio of the debtor's income. In the case of Greece, its *debt to GDP ratio rose by 50 percentage points* over the decade: from 127 percent in 2009 to 177 percent in 2019. Why? Not principally because of the growth of debt, but *because Greece grew dramatically poorer* over the course of the austerity program. Its GDP declined by 21 percent, from €238 billion to €187 billion. An international team of leading "mainstream" economists termed this "an output collapse unprecedented in the annals of modern Europe."[177]

Not only can economists understand perfectly well the concept of "debt dynamics"—namely, that if the interest rate on debt is higher than the growth rate of income (in the case of a nation, its GDP growth rate, on which depends the growth of tax revenues), the debtor will sink deeper into debt—but so can any layperson. In Greece's case, the growth rate of GDP is *negative*.

The IMF projects that Greece will return to its 2010 GDP in 2034 (as shown by the dotted line in the following chart), the sort of fantasy projection that can only be made by IMF economists.[178]

In fact, the leading economies did not lose money as a result of the Greek crisis. Their gain, due to the reduction in their own borrowing costs (as international investors in government bonds shifted from Greece and other weak economies to dominant economies like the United States, United Kingdom, Japan, and Germany), outweighed what they provided toward the Greek bailouts.[179] Thus, they would remain net gainers even if they were never repaid a cent. Nevertheless, in exchange for the bailouts, they imposed a regime of austerity on Greece *in perpetuity*: the EU's plan for Greece's rehabilitation envisions that it will continue to generate primary budget surpluses of 3.5 percent of GDP until 2023 and then 2 percent of GDP until *2060* (!).[180] Thus, future generations of Greeks are to remain in debtors' prison.

In 2010, the IMF confidently projected that, once Greece submitted

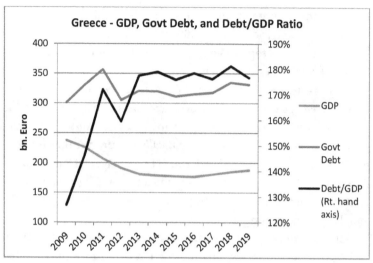

Source: Compiled from Statistical Data Warehouse, European Central Bank, available at
sdw.ecb.europa.eu.

to the IMF and EU, "real GDP growth is expected to contract
sharply in 2010–11 and recover thereafter. Growth is expected
to follow a V-shaped pattern: the frontloaded fiscal contraction
in 2010–11 will suppress domestic demand in the short run; but
from 2012 onward, confidence effects, regained market access, and
comprehensive structural reforms are expected to lead to a growth
recovery."[181]

It is worth keeping in mind that Indian officials today also predict
a "V-shaped recovery."

At the IMF board meeting in 2010, which decided on the Greek
bailout, many countries were opposed and thought debts should be
cancelled instead. However, these were third world countries whose
opinions carried little weight:

Most strikingly, drawing on their own experience of failed bailouts in the late 1990s and early 2000s, Argentina argued that a
"debt restructuring should have been on the table". Brazil said
the IMF loans: "may be seen not as a rescue of Greece, which

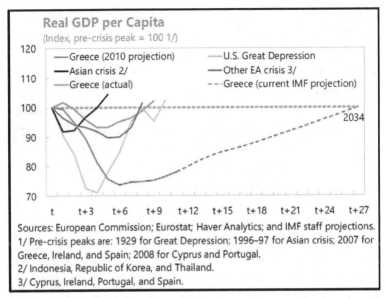

Sources: European Commission; Eurostat; Haver Analytics; and IMF staff projections.
1/ Pre-crisis peaks are: 1929 for Great Depression; 1996–97 for Asian crisis; 2007 for Greece, Ireland, and Spain; 2008 for Cyprus and Portugal.
2/ Indonesia, Republic of Korea, and Thailand.
3/ Cyprus, Ireland, Portugal, and Spain.

Source: *Greece: Staff Report for the 2019 Article IV Consultation* (Washington DC: International Monetary Fund, 2019). "t+3," "t+6," and so on, refer to the number of years from the starting point. The peak GDP before the crisis is taken as 100, and the remaining years are mapped as ratios of that peak GDP. As can be seen, the Greek crisis finds no parallel.

will have to undergo a wrenching adjustment, but as a bailout of Greece's private debt holders, mainly European financial institutions."

Iran said it would have expected a debt restructure to be discussed, as did Egypt, which said the IMF's growth projections were "optimistic," a word repeated by China.[182]

Particularly interesting, from our point of view, was the view of India's representative at the board meeting: "India warned that the scale of cuts would start a spiral of falling unemployment which would reduce government revenue, causing the debt to increase, and making a future debt restructuring inevitable."[183]

When we discuss India's current policy, we can look back at this pertinent advice.

In 2010, the IMF anticipated that GDP by 2013, at €235 billion, would exceed 2010 levels (€231 billion). However, by 2013, the Greek economy had in fact shrunk 20 percent. In 2013, IMF economists acknowledged that they had grossly underestimated the impact that government spending cuts and tax hikes would have on economic activity, employment, and investment in those European countries that were subjected to austerity programs.[184] The outstanding example of this was Greece. However, this research finding brought no relief to Greece. Its austerity program continued on the basis of the earlier (and now invalidated) forecasts. In 2013, the troika forecast that Greece's public debt to GDP ratio would fall to 124 percent by 2020, underestimating the eventual figure by over 50 percent.

As the explicitly intended result of the troika program, Greece's wage levels declined steeply: private sector nominal wages decreased by about 20 percent from 2010. But the promised "pay off" from this horrendous sacrifice never came. The drop in wages was meant to lead to a growth in jobs, since workers were now cheaper, but instead, as the IMF acknowledges, "Greece continues to have the highest rate [of unemployment] in the Euro Area, with long-term unemployment [as a percentage of total unemployment] persistently above 60 percent for the last five years and youth unemployment at 40 percent (also the highest in the region)."[185]

The combination of falling wages and rising unemployment meant greater poverty. The IMF notes that "working age Greeks face greater 'at risk of poverty' than pensioners." It recommends reducing old-age pensions as a way of overcoming this anomaly, so that pensioners can join the young in poverty.[186] Indeed, pension cuts are a key element to the "reform" measures the IMF is pressing on Greece.

According to Organisation for Economic Co-operation and Development measures, poverty in Greece doubled between 2009 and 2018.[187] The World Bank puts "multidimensional poverty" in Greece at 31.8 percent in 2018.[188]

Greece for Sale

A key objective of the EU has been to push through the privatization program. This is done in the name of reducing the debt—thus, European Commission president Jean-Claude Juncker said in 2015 that Greece could make €50 billion from asset sales.[189] At the European Union summit in July 2015, German finance minister, Wolfgang Schäuble, rejected Greece's offer of raising €500 million through privatizations every year and told the media: "I said €50 billion, €50 billion!"[190]

However, it was pure fiction that privatization would ever reduce Greece's debt. According to the IMF, between 2008 and 2018, Greece's privatization proceeds contributed a reduction of the public debt by 1.3 percent. The IMF projects that, between 2019 and 2028, privatization would contribute to reducing the public debt another 1.2 percent.[191] Hence, the purpose of privatization is not to reduce the debt, but rather to use the debt to force Greece to part with its assets, yielding a jackpot for foreign investors.

Privatization will *necessarily* be at undervalued, depressed prices. First, these sales are being carried out in distress conditions, when the seller is under pressure to meet certain targets, but the buyers are under no such pressure to buy. In order to ensure the "success" of the sale, the sellers deliberately undervalue the asset. Second, there is no real competitive bidding. Domestic firms are in no financial condition to bid and international bidders for such large assets are few. Third, as we shall see, the beneficiaries have their representatives on the board of the very agency doing the selling.

After 2010, the Greek government recapitalized the country's four major private banks, the National Bank of Greece, Piraeus Bank, Alpha Bank, and Eurobank, using public funds. On this basis, it was logical to have nationalized them. Instead, their shares were sold at "ridiculously low" prices to U.S. and other foreign hedge funds (speculative investment funds).[192]

As a result public ownership of banks has been dramatically reduced, the public sums previously given to banks for recapitalisation have effectively evaporated, and international hedge funds have acquired significant equity stakes in Greek banks. Under these conditions it is highly unlikely that there would be a strong revival of bank credit in the foreseeable future.[193]

Thereafter, the four banks have been selling the "non-performing loans" (that is, bad debt) since 2017. The buyers of the loans would get control of the assets of the borrowers. This was the next act of denationalization: "The bank privatization facilitated the seizure of private property of Greek businesses through the 'red loans' and securities held by the banks. . . . Small and medium enterprise seizures came next, and included primary residences."[194]

That is, people's homes were also seized. A U.S. Department of State website on the investment climate in Greece notes that "the potential sale and/or transfer of Greek NPLs [non-performing loans] continues to receive interest by a large number of Greek and foreign companies and funds."[195]

In 2011, the Greek government set up the Hellenic Republic Asset Development Fund and turned over to it listed and unlisted state-owned enterprises, infrastructure (including thirty-five ports, forty airports, and the natural gas company), buildings, three thousand pieces of real estate, national monuments, national roads, and the military industry. However, the EU was dissatisfied with the progress of the fund. As a condition of the 2015 bailout, the Hellenic Corporation for Assets and Participation was set up, with a lifespan of ninety-nine years, and all assets of the Hellenic Republic Asset Development Fund were turned over to it. The board of the Hellenic Corporation for Assets and Participation consists of three persons nominated by the Greek government and two, including the chairperson, selected by the EU and the European Stability Mechanism. The foreign lenders are now satisfied that privatization is moving ahead, with the privatization of ports at Piraeus and Thessaloniki, ten regional ports and marinas, and the fourteen busiest airports in the country. The sale of power corporation units, the natural gas company, and Greece's biggest highway are reportedly underway.

One example suffices to illustrate the process underway. The Fraport consortium, headed by the German airport Frankfurt, will pay €1.23 billion for Greece's fourteen busiest regional airports—amounting to the net income the Greek government gets from these airports in just three years. (Minus the expenditure recently incurred by the Greek government on these airports, the sale will amount to just €714 million.) In forty years, Fraport is projected to earn €22 billion from these airports, but pay a rental of €3.85 billion to Greece.[196]

6

Deepening Dependence and Uncertainty

In chapter 4, we saw that the government's refusal to undertake public spending in response to the COVID-19 epidemic stems from its anxiety to woo foreign financial investors. Foreign investors, in general, are strongly opposed to increased government spending by third world countries.

In the previous chapter, we explained why foreign investors generally oppose third world countries' government spending: reducing government spending leaves the field open for private capital to set its terms and enables private investors to extract all sorts of concessions and giveaways as the price of investment. That is, foreign investors especially stand to gain when government spending is kept down. In the present situation, it is foreign investors and a handful of the top Indian capitalists who are best positioned to take advantage of these opportunities.

We showed how the economic collapse triggered by COVID-19 and the rulers' refusal to spend are helping usher in a major restructuring of India's economy in favor of foreign capital (even though the restructuring had in fact begun *before* the virus entered India).

The Course Taken

In response to a crisis such as the present one, any government today is faced with a choice. On the one hand, it could defy the pressure of global finance and address the basic needs of the people of the country (which is within the reach of India's material capacity—a fact that is particularly glaring now, when there are substantial food stocks, unutilized industrial capacity, and low oil prices). To take this course, however, the government would need to impose controls on flows of foreign capital and prepare to forgo future such inflows of foreign capital (with all that this implies) in order to pursue a course of democratic national development.

On the other hand, such a government may instead submit to the regime of foreign finance, awaiting signals on how much to spend at different junctures (and on what), thereby giving up any pretense to economic sovereignty. India's rulers have adhered to this latter course of submission.

Even though the 2003–08 credit boom in India left the economy laden with a great deadweight of external and domestic debt, and even though the world economy is in a state of great uncertainty and gloom, India's rulers are set on expanding the country's foreign liabilities in ways that will make the country more vulnerable to dictation and pressure. Here, we look at how this drive is deepening India's foreign dependence and economic instability.

Relentless Drive to Attract Foreign Inflows

We have to keep in mind that the U.S. dollar, the currency of the leading imperialist country and military power, continues to be the principal global currency. The majority of world trade is conducted in dollars and the bulk of the foreign exchange reserves held by central banks the world over are in the form of dollar assets. The dollar is also a "safe haven" in any storm for the big wealth holders of the world: whenever there is a global crisis, even one that originates in or is centers in the United States itself, investors worldwide shift their investments *into* dollars. As they sell other currencies and buy dollars, the other currencies, particularly the currencies of developing countries, fall in value. This means that imports into the developing countries become more expensive in local currency terms. Therefore, countries try to maintain an ample supply of dollars in order to stave off a crisis.

In India's case, there is a seeming contradiction:

It would seem, the country is not facing any foreign exchange crisis. The foreign investors in India's stock market who exited in March 2020 have returned with a bang (buying in, no doubt, at lower prices!). More significantly, foreign investors have been buying up Indian *firms*, or parts thereof, as we described in the previous chapter. Thus, these funds too are now flowing in. Indeed, from the end of 2019 to July 31, 2020, the foreign exchange reserves have risen by about $75 billion to $535 billion.

But, despite this vast mountain of reserves, the government is making desperate efforts to gather additional foreign inflows and sources of dollars, as if to protect against a foreign exchange crisis. No doubt the rulers are acutely sensitive to the fact that India's foreign exchange reserves consist of *borrowings*, much of which can flow out on short notice in any seeming emergency.

In their effort to shore up the reserves, they are currently focused on two objectives: (1) attracting foreign investment into Indian "government debt" and (2) trying to obtain "swap lines" from the U.S. central bank (the Federal Reserve).

Both have grave consequences, which are being passed over virtually without objection or comment.

Wooing Foreign Investment into Government Bonds

The government attempts to justify the wooing of foreign investment into government bonds as a way of easing the government's funds crunch. This is a bogus argument (for reasons we explain in the endnote, "Bogus Argument to Justify Wooing Foreign Investment into Government Debt"). It will not provide any additional resources, but will merely pile up further external debt to fickle investors who can withdraw their investments at any time, such as when interest rates somewhere else seem more attractive. The government has chosen the hour of the country's gravest economic crisis to place the economy at the mercy of "bond tourists."

The story of this courtship of bond tourists begins earlier. The first step the finance minister took in this direction had to be abandoned. Finance Minister Sitharaman announced in the July 2019 Union Budget that "the government would start raising a part of its gross borrowing programme in external markets in external currencies."[197] Since such borrowings would be priced not in rupees, but in dollars or some other foreign currency, any fall in the value of the rupee vis-à-vis that currency would increase the burden of debt servicing (that is, we would have to pay more rupees).

This led to strenuous objections even by economists who are otherwise in favor of liberalization and globalization, since they are aware that a large number of countries that have funded their government spending in such a fashion have come to grief in the past: their debt-servicing costs suddenly soared when their currencies depreciated and entire economies spun into crisis. In the face of criticism from unexpected quarters, the Indian government retreated for the moment on the proposal to issue dollar-denominated debt. But it did not give up on its plan to attract foreign investors to government debt; it merely turned to soliciting their entry into rupee-denominated debt.

Shepherding India into Global Bond Indices

In September 2018, Prime Minister Modi met the billionaire Michael Bloomberg in New York. Bloomberg, head of the giant financial firm Bloomberg L.P., promised to shepherd India to be included in global indices of government bonds.

> Together with the Indian Ministry of Finance, Reserve Bank of India, Securities and Exchange Board of India and key financial institutions, Bloomberg will work with India to navigate the

process to gain inclusion in global benchmark indices to significantly increase the country's ability to attract capital to its bond markets. These indices have traditionally helped countries attract foreign capital, but required significant, time-intensive reforms at the local level. Bloomberg will, among other actions, convene senior Indian officials and investors from prominent financial centers to solicit feedback and diverse perspectives needed to enhance India's bond markets.[198]

These "indices" consist of baskets of government bonds from around the world, such as the Bloomberg Global Bond Index Fund and the JP Morgan Global EM Index. In each index, different bonds take up more or less space depending on the value they represent.[199] The Indian government argues that many large international funds invest passively, automatically distributing their investments in proportion to the composition of the index. Hence, they claim that India's inclusion in such an index would lead to a certain percentage of global funds automatically flowing to Indian government bonds.

Foreign investors at present hold less than 4 percent of India's outstanding government debt. Bloomberg's India economist says inclusion in benchmark indices could mean that upward of $50 billion to $125 billion would flow into India immediately—that is, perhaps an additional 2.5 to 6.5 percent of government debt, as a start.

Freedom of Capital to Enter and Exit

The proposal to get India listed in global bond indices is not new. It has been under discussion since at least 2013. However, at the time, the government and the RBI felt it was too risky to take the steps required. Prerequisites to enter such indices include removing all caps, controls, and quotas on foreign investment in government bonds and, eventually, on corporate bonds as well. Foreign investors in rupee-denominated bonds would also want to hedge their investment against a depreciation in the rupee's exchange rate, and so trading in India's foreign exchange markets would have to be opened up to foreign investors. In essence, what international markets demand is that India move further toward what is called full "capital account convertibility" —the free movement of capital in and out of the country, into and out of any domestic assets.

This would open up India further to volatility. Even today, external events (such as changes in U.S. interest rates) or a sudden loss of foreign confidence in the Indian economy lead to rapid outflows, destabilizing the economy. India experienced rapid outflows for brief spells in 2008, 2013, and March 2020. But this destabilizing impact would be multiplied with full capital account convertibility. Full capital account convertibility is the same path that south and east Asian countries traveled before 1997, resulting in the devastating crisis of 1997 and 1998 in those countries.

In fact, until 1997, the Indian government and the RBI were charting a course to full capital account convertibility for India, but they retreated after the Asian crisis. To date, India has only partial capital account convertibility. Such has been the worldwide experience of destabilizing capital flows that even the IMF, long the high priest of capital account convertibility, has been forced to admit (grudgingly and with many caveats) that capital account convertibility may cause harm and that placing controls on capital movements can play a positive role in some circumstances.

Apart from capital account convertibility, global bond indices will expect tight controls on government spending in India and ruthless suppression of inflation (by suppressing domestic demand and keeping down wages and crop procurement prices—that is, deflating the incomes of workers and peasants).

In fact, *the government's refusal to spend even during the present dire economic and public health crisis can partly be explained by its anxiety to get listed on global bond indices* and to display its adherence to principles of fiscal austerity.

Until March 30, 2020, foreign investment in Indian government debt was permitted, but with various restrictions, such as a cap of 6 percent of total government debt. On March 30, while the attention of the country was focused on the COVID-19 crisis, the RBI issued a notification opening certain specified categories of government debt securities fully for foreign investors. This is only the first step, as more and more securities will be added to the fully accessible route.

The Myth of Stability

The government claims that being included in global bond indices will provide a stable flow of foreign investment, which is not subject to sudden fluctuations. However, this is not true. For example, take Indonesia, where 30 to 40 percent of government debt is held by foreigners. Indonesia is prominent in global indices of "emerging market" government debt. Nevertheless, in 2013 and 2018, Indonesia experienced rollercoaster rides. This was for no reason of its domestic economy, but merely because the U.S. central bank, the Federal Reserve, discussed raising *its* interest rates, whereupon foreign investors in Indonesian government debt started moving capital back to the United States, setting off a series of other consequences.

Given the lightning speed with which funds can move out, once foreign investors hold a sizable share of Indian government debt, the Indian government will have to be permanently on its "best behavior," keeping government spending low and doing other things to please foreign investors.

Remarkably, this momentous development has taken place almost entirely without critical comment or even scrutiny. Virtually the only critical note was sounded by the former governor of the RBI, Urjit Patel, in April: "Last week, our breathless pursuit for being part of global bond indices gathered pace. Over the past year, we have incessantly relaxed prudential norms related to external flows management, opening up yet more the possibilities of surges and sudden stops of 'hot' foreign capital with well-known attendant consequences." He warned that by opening up to foreign investors in government debt, *"we are opening the capital account for 'bond tourists' further."*[200] The warning has gone unheeded.

The general silence on this question is all the more curious considering that the earlier (July 2019) proposal to issue dollar-denominated government debt invited sharp criticism, even from pro-liberalization economists. The present step avoids certain risks in the earlier proposal, but similarly exposes India to dangerous volatility from foreign investors. Perhaps the measure was ignored because it was taken at the height of the COVID-19 lockdown, amid a flight of capital and an all-enveloping sense of crisis. The present COVID-19-related crisis, so to speak, has lent cover to the germination of a future crisis.

The Quest for Swap Lines

Apart from soliciting foreign investment in government debt, the Indian government is appealing to the United States for help in the form of swap lines. A currency swap line is an agreement between two central banks to exchange a certain amount of their respective currencies for a fixed period. The U.S. Federal Reserve would provide the RBI a certain amount of dollars in exchange for rupees on a particular date, at the exchange rate prevailing on that date. Six months later, the two banks would return to each other the same amounts of each other's currencies, even if the rupee's exchange rate against the dollar had changed in the interim. The RBI would also pay the U.S. Federal Reserve a rate of interest, although developed world central banks would get dollars interest free.

The benefit would be that the RBI would get dollars quickly without approaching the IMF (which would impose conditions). Moreover, even if the rupee fell in value against the dollar in the interim, the RBI would not face any additional burdens. (The need for dollars may arise, say, if the RBI has to help out the Indian corporate sector, which has borrowed vast sums abroad recently, apparently without insuring itself against a fall in the rupee.)

The United States announced that its existing swap lines with Canada, England, Japan, the European Central Bank, and Switzerland would be unlimited—that is, that they could draw as many dollars as they needed. On March 19, 2020, it extended *limited* swap lines to another nine countries: Australia, Sweden, Denmark, Norway, New Zealand, Singapore, South Korea, Brazil, and Mexico. India has kept trying to get a swap line, but has not succeeded so far.[201]

Why do countries suffer a shortfall of dollars and need swap lines or IMF loans? Because, in many cases, they have earlier been subjected to a flood of dollars. These floods have resulted in huge debts that the recipient countries have to service and may have to repay on short notice. Developing countries all remember the Asian crisis of 1997–98 and are determined to protect themselves from a repetition. Hence, over one hundred countries have approached the IMF for loans since the beginning of the COVID-19 crisis.

The "Apartheid" of Swap Lines

It is worth looking back at a speech delivered in 2017 by Patel as RBI governor, in which he spelled out the context in which swap lines were anxiously sought by developing countries. He pointed out that it was the economic policies of the *advanced* economies and their central banks, massively expanding credit at near-zero interest rates, that

> have been the main push factors driving the influx of capital flows to EMEs [emerging market economies]. For these recipient economies, this has translated into heightened financial market volatility with adverse implications for their growth prospects and for macroeconomic and financial stability. . . . As high intensity events starting with the taper tantrum have shown, macroeconomic fundamentals do not matter in the face of these large and sudden movements of capital, and their economies remain vulnerable to rapid materialization of risks.
>
> So far, our quest for a robust, equitable and quickly deployable global financial safety net has remained elusive. . . . Given the "stigma" attached to the IMF facilities and their quest for "self-insurance", EMEs have resorted to building foreign exchange reserves as the "first line of defence" to calm volatility

in financial markets and to provide adequate liquidity buffers for "sudden stop" and reversals. . . .

With every new tail event, however, the churn becomes larger, the volatility ever higher, threatening to overwhelm the modest defences that EMEs are able to muster.

During the Global Financial Crisis of 2007–09 and since then, the U.S. central bank dramatically expanded bilateral swap lines with other central banks. But it kept these swaps within a narrow circle of advanced economies. Patel termed this practice a virtual "apartheid":

> It is in this context that I would draw your attention to the stark asymmetry prevailing in the provision of swap lines by systemic central banks. In fact, I would go as far as describing the situation as a virtual "apartheid" by which systemic central banks [the central banks of the world's leading economies] protect themselves and their self-interest. Meanwhile, EMEs [emerging market economies] that are at the receiving end of global financial turbulence are systematically denied access. . . . We must learn from the lessons of the global financial crisis and act expeditiously and comprehensively to establish a broader swap network.[202]

The United States did not respond then to these pleas.

The cries for a global financial safety net have grown louder since the onset of the COVID-19 crisis. As the United Nations Conference on Trade and Development pointed out in March 2020, capital has flowed out of the developing countries, their international borrowing costs have risen, the prices of their export commodities have fallen (their export revenues are projected to fall $800 billion in 2020), and their currency values have depreciated, all to a much greater extent than during the Global Financial Crisis. Under these circumstances, the developing countries will be hard put to make external debt payments of $1.62 trillion in 2020 and $1.08 trillion in 2021. The United Nations Conference on Trade and Development remarked: "In the current dollar-centric global system, the United States' Federal Reserve can extend its role as lender of last resort beyond the country's borders but it currently does so in a strategic way which favours a select group [of] countries."[203]

Swap lines give the United States the power of financial life and death over countries short of dollars, and it intends to use this strategic lever to the fullest.

A Shift in the Approach to Addressing the Global Crisis

In 2008, the United States and its allies decided to address the Global Financial Crisis by going beyond the G-7 group of leading economies and convening the G-20 group. The latter included China and some major developing countries, such as India, Saudi Arabia, South Africa, Brazil, Indonesia, Mexico, and Turkey. A recent World Bank study says that, in the wake of the 2008 crisis, "emerging markets and developing economies" received

> large, prompt, and global policy support. Coordinated by the G20, the largest advanced economies and EMDEs [emerging markets and developing economies] implemented unprecedented monetary and fiscal stimulus in 2009 and 2010. EMDE governments employed fiscal packages that included infrastructure investment, tax cuts, and social protection programs. EMDE central banks lowered policy interest rates.[204]

The IMF was given additional resources and was also permitted to issue fresh special drawing rights worth $250 billion.

Special drawing rights are, for all practical purposes, a type of global money that the IMF is authorized to create. Since special drawing rights can be traded for specific currencies, countries can use them to settle their international payments of debt or imports. Each fresh issue of special drawing rights is distributed to all IMF member countries according to their respective shareholdings. They get this without conditions and without incurring any debt.

There is a clear shift from the U.S. approach to the 2008 crisis to its approach to the present one. The reason for this shift must be seen in light of the fact that, despite the unprecedented stimulus packages in the United States and elsewhere, there was no full-fledged recovery from the 2007–09 crisis, even in the developed world. Indeed, the world economy was poised to reenter a recession in 2020 *even if* COVID-19 had not come about. As the cake became smaller, the tussles for crumbs cake grew sharper. U.S.-China trade disputes repeatedly neared the breaking point.

In the earlier crisis, the United States and its allies were anxious to rescue their giant financial firms and revive growth (in however distorted a fashion). They therefore wanted all countries to increase their spending. This time, in 2020, developing countries have not been given such a "free pass" to increase spending. Despite the much more severe blow to economic activity, the fiscal packages announced by virtually all the developing countries in the wake of COVID-19 are in the low single digits as percentages of their respective GDPs. Meanwhile, the United States sees little stake in reviving global demand and is instead preoccupied with its anti-China agenda. For example, a day before the virtual G-20 summit, the foreign ministers of the G-7 were unable to agree on a joint statement because of U.S. insistence on labeling, in a racist manner, COVID-19 the "Wuhan virus."[205]

Why India Voted with the United States and Against Its Own Interests

With the COVID-19 crisis, the United Nations Conference on Trade and Development as well as other prominent political bodies called for the IMF to issue fresh special drawing rights equivalent to $1 trillion. The IMF eventually proposed just $500 billion worth of special drawing rights. Had the proposal passed, the developing countries would have received 40 percent of the total. However, the United States has a 16.5 percent share in the IMF and an 85 percent vote is required for certain decisions, such as on special drawing rights. Thus, the United States simply blocked the proposal.

The U.S. vote is not surprising, since the country wants to extract many pounds of flesh for any relief given and a special drawing rights issue would provide some relief without allowing such gouging. What is remarkable is that *India too voted against* the proposed issuance of special drawing rights (it appears to have been the only country to have joined the United States in this), *even though it would have been a beneficiary had the proposal passed.*[206] Of course, the U.S. vote alone would have been sufficient to block the proposal, but the Indian rulers decided to display their dependability to the United States by voting with it. They presumably hoped that the United States would reward this poodle-like conduct with the equivalent of a biscuit and a pat on the head.

However, two months have passed since then and the United States has still not extended swap lines to India. If India persists in its attempts and the United States finally agrees to extend it a line, the latter will no doubt extract as much as it can get in return. The *quid pro quo* may not be purely financial; it may be strategic as well.

ENDNOTE: BOGUS ARGUMENT TO JUSTIFY WOOING FOREIGN INVESTMENT INTO GOVERNMENT DEBT

The government attempts to justify the wooing of foreign investment into government debt as a way of easing the government's funds crunch. Its argument is that India can "tap foreign savings" and give the economy a boost.

This argument is spurious. In order to "tap more foreign savings," India would have to expand its external current account deficit correspondingly (the current account is the broadest measure of its trade balance and includes net services income and net investment income). Such a policy is not in the cards. Rather, the greater dependence on such foreign investment in government debt would result in a steady bleeding of the economy. Let us illustrate the falsity of the government's argument with a simple example.

An Analogy

Imagine a person, Sharda, whose expenditure is ₹50,000 more than her earnings and who, therefore, needs a loan to cover the difference. However, for some reason, she receives a loan of ₹100,000, which is more than she needs. She deposits the remaining ₹50,000 in the bank, where, unfortunately, it earns a lower rate of interest than she is paying on the loan.

Does it make sense for Sharda to take out more loans at this point? Evidently not.

Let us apply this analogy to India's external accounts. India's earnings from abroad (exports of goods and services, and remittances by Indian workers abroad) are less than what it pays foreigners (imports of goods and services, and payments on foreign debt and investments). These recurring earnings and payments are called the *current account*; the deficit in this account (between earnings and payments) is called the *current account deficit*.

This gap has to be covered by net inflows of capital (borrowings and foreign investments). These one-time flows are called the *capital account* and, when the inflows are more than the outflows on the capital account, we get a *capital account surplus*.

However, just as Sharda received a bigger loan than she needed, India's capital account surplus is usually larger than its current account deficit. And just as Sharda had to deposit the extra amount in the bank, when India gets a capital account surplus larger than its current account deficit, the excess sum winds up in India's foreign exchange reserves. These reserves are invested abroad, for example, in U.S. government bonds, which earn very low interest rates, much lower than the rates paid on Indian government rupee bonds. This amounts to a drain from India.

It is in this situation that the government is at present soliciting *additional* foreign investment in government debt. As we have seen, in the present conditions, the government's justification for this—that it is tapping foreign savings for India's development—is nonsense.

Theoretically, if India were to jack up its imports and run a much larger current account deficit, it could absorb these additional foreign capital inflows. But to do so would be positively harmful to economic activity in India. Moreover, foreign investors take a rising current account deficit—anything above, say, 3 percent of GDP—as a sign of unsustainably high consumption in India, and hence of an impending crisis. This itself would lead to a panic outflow of foreign investments, stock market crash, and fall in the rupee's exchange rate. Therefore, the government is not really contemplating a policy of expanding the current account deficit.

When foreign investors invest in Indian government securities, that is, when they lend to the Indian government, they earn an interest rate in rupees, which they then convert to dollars at the prevailing exchange rate and remit home. If the exchange rate remains steady, they face no worries. However, if, during a crisis, the rupee's exchange rate were to fall, such foreign investors in government debt would convert their interest earnings from rupees to dollars at the now reduced exchange rate, remitting less dollars home. As a result, in any period of crisis, foreign investors in government securities might sell off their holdings in a hurry, and thereby intensify the crisis.

Thus, what is on the cards is merely that, as foreign investors invest in Indian government debt, any excess foreign capital inflows will swell the already-large foreign exchange reserves. India's large foreign exchange reserves would give the impression of greater security on the external front and reassure foreign investors of repayment. At the same time, any such inflows are also foreign liabilities, meaning, what we owe foreigners. And, of course, foreign investors in government debt can sell their investments at the press of a button—indeed they withdrew $8 billion in just one month, March 2020. The entire exercise thrusts India deeper into dependence and uncertainty.

7

India, COVID-19, the United States, and China

On May 5, 2020, in the middle of India's COVID-related lockdown, tensions began building between Indian and Chinese troops at various points along the Line of Actual Control, the de facto frontier between India and China. Finally, on the night of June 15, the two sides clashed in hand-to-hand combat on the slopes of the Galwan Valley. Twenty Indian troops died, as did an unknown number of their Chinese counterparts. This was the most serious clash between the two armies since the war of 1962.

The clash took place in a region of strategic importance. On the Chinese side of the Galwan Valley lies Aksai Chin, through which a key road connects Tibet and Xinjiang province. On the Indian side, to the west, lies Ladakh. Further west from Ladakh is Pakistan-administered Gilgit-Baltistan, through which runs the China-Pakistan Economic Corridor, a belt of infrastructural projects extending in the south to Pakistan's port of Gwadar. China-Pakistan Economic Corridor pipelines would give China more secure access to Gulf oil and gas, avoiding U.S. naval patrols in southeast Asia.

China may view recent steps by India—such as the August 2019 decision to carve out Ladakh and make it a centrally administered territory, as well as the buildup of Indian military infrastructure in Ladakh, near the Line of Actual Control—as strategic threats.

Taking India's side, U.S. Secretary of State Mike Pompeo said the clashes were "initiated by the PLA" [People's Liberation Army] and "are just the latest examples of the CCP's [Chinese Communist Party] unacceptable behaviour. . . . The United States has never been more supportive of India's security. India too, is an important partner and a key pillar of President [Donald] Trump's foreign policy."[207]

Within India, the border standoff triggered an uproar. Politicians and sundry celebrities called for a boycott of all Chinese goods; government bodies canceled Chinese contracts; and, on June 29, 2020, India's Ministry of Electronics and Information Technology banned fifty-nine Chinese apps, some of which, like TikTok, had a large number of users in India. Pompeo welcomed India's ban, claiming that these apps "can serve as appendages of the CCP's surveillance state."[208] While hostilities at the Line of Actual Control have ceased for the time being, they have had a more lasting impact on India's domestic political climate and foreign policy stance.

On the surface, then, it appears as if a deadly physical brawl in the Himalayas somehow snowballed into a struggle in the spheres of commerce and strategic affairs. To look beneath the surface, let us first place these events in their global context.

The Uses of the COVID-19 Crisis

In the period since the emergence of COVID-19, the United States has quite openly decided to use the crisis, at a global scale, as a weapon against its perceived rival, China. As early as January 30, 2020, just days after the confirmation of human-to-human transmission of the virus, the U.S. Commerce Secretary said that the disease, while "very unfortunate," could prompt companies to reconsider operating inside China. This was not an off-the-cuff remark. The Commerce Department followed up with an e-mail stating: "It is also important to consider the ramifications of doing business with a country that has a long history of covering up real risks to its own people and the rest of the world."

On April 9, Japan announced that it would subsidize its firms if they moved their production base from China.[209] The European Union is preparing a report claiming that "China has continued to run a global disinformation campaign to deflect blame for the outbreak of the pandemic and improve its international image."[210] The French President Emmanuel Macron has questioned China's handling of the virus outbreak.[211] The European Commission chief has asked for an investigation into the origins of the virus.[212] And, of course, the U.S. President has pressed U.S. intelligence agencies to find the source of the virus, threatening in his distinctive manner to sue China $10 million for every U.S. COVID-related death.[213]

This chorus has *little to do with the virus, except its use as an opportunity.* The process was under way well before COVID-19. The attempt to diversify global manufacturing chains away from China has been under discussion for the past two years, particularly in the wake of the U.S.-China trade conflict.

A Different Type of Globalization

In the period between 1990 and 2008, the globalization of production proceeded at breakneck speed, and an estimated 70 percent of global trade now involves global value chains. However, a special report by the *Economist* in July 2019 (long before COVID-19) found "a slow unravelling" of these chains. "A survey conducted in April [2019] of 600 MNCs [multinational corporations] around Asia by Baker McKenzie, an American law firm, found that nearly half of them are considering 'major' changes to their supply chains, and over a tenth a complete overhaul. In many sectors this will mean a rethink of the role that China plays in sourcing."[214]

McKinsey Global Institute finds that global value chains in sixteen of seventeen big industries it has studied have become shorter, often moving production closer to the targeted consumer markets. This does not necessarily mean an end to globalization, but a shift in its pattern—for example, shifting production to other low-wage countries: "The [U.S.-China] trade war has also led to a rethink at Apple, which has reportedly asked its biggest suppliers to see how much it would cost to shift 15–30% of its supply base out of China to South-East Asia or India."[215]

However, it is not easy for multinational firms to leave China—half the world's electronics-manufacturing capacity is based there and the country offers advantages in infrastructure, skills, scale, and agility that are not easily matched. Nevertheless, significantly, the *Economist* report concludes that "Trump's economic nationalism and attacks on China have won over America's corporate elite. . . . There is bound to be an acceleration in the slow unravelling that is already under way of the complex supply chains that linked China to America."[216]

Huawei Targeted

In 2019, more trade restrictions have been placed on China than on any other country. In the wake of the pandemic, a number of countries have placed restrictions on Chinese investment in their countries, as if in retaliation for the virus.[217] A particular target of restrictions and bans has been the Chinese telecom giant Huawei.

Huawei, China's largest private capitalist corporation, is widely considered to have the best and cheapest 5G technology, which would in the normal course be installed throughout the world. Precisely for this reason, U.S. pressure on Huawei is intense. In December 2018, Canada arrested Meng Wanzhou, the chief financial officer of Huawei, on an extradition request from the United States. In May 2020, the United States required foreign semiconductor manufacturers exporting to Huawei to seek permission from the United States if any U.S. equipment or software were involved in the manufacture.

As a result, the United Kingdom finally scrapped its decision to involve Huawei in setting up its 5G networks, resulting in up to two years' delay and an additional cost of £2 billion. UK telecom firms have been given until 2027 to rip out existing Huawei gear from their networks. The remaining members of the Five Eyes (the communications surveillance alliance comprising the United States, United Kingdom, Canada, Australia, and New Zealand) have de facto bans

Breakdown of Countries on Allowing Huawei to Operate

Position	Countries
Open to Huawei	China; Malaysia
Permitted, but not in sensitive parts of the network	Netherlands
Unlikely to consider restrictions	Latin America; Central America; Africa; Russia
Considering Restrictions	Belgium; Norway; Germany; Czech Republic; Italy
Soft Restrictions	Poland; Taiwan; South Korea
Hard Restrictions	United States; Britain; France; Israel; Japan; Australia; New Zealand
Undecided	Afghanistan; Bangladesh; Denmark; Greece; Indonesia; Iran; Ireland; Kazakhstan; Myanmar; Pakistan; Philippines; Saudi Arabia; Tajikistan; Turkmenistan; Uzbekistan; Vietnam

Source: Updated based on the map "For or Against Huawei," *Economist*, July 13, 2019.

on Huawei. France too has imposed a de facto ban on Huawei, which will result in the phasing out of the Chinese firm's equipment by 2028 at the latest.[218] Germany is stepping down its purchases from Huawei, but has not yet banned them.

The initial justification for these measures was so-called security concerns—the possibility of China using Huawei 5G equipment to spy on Western powers. But U.S. sanctions forced the hand of several countries and actual commercial concerns are impossible to separate from the strategic motives. The drive to capture or retain markets and sources of raw material, and to deny them to one's rivals, is a staple of imperialist strategy. The UK prime minister, Boris Johnson, has now approached the United States to form a "D-10" club of "democracies," consisting of the Group of 7 (the United States, United Kingdom, Germany, France, Japan, Italy, and Canada, with observer status for the European Union) plus Australia, South Korea, and India. The addition of the last three indicates that the grouping is focused on China. *The Times* (London) reports that the first activity of this grouping would be to wrest markets from its rival: "One option would see the club channel investment to technology companies based within

its member states. Nokia and Ericsson are the only European suppliers of 5G infrastructure and experts say that they cannot provide 5G
kit as quickly or cheaply as Huawei."[219]

The Economist predicts that "the Huawei fallout could lead to the
bifurcation of global markets into two incompatible 5G camps.... In
this scenario, Sweden's Ericsson, Finland's Nokia and South Korea's
Samsung would supply a pricier network comprised of kit made outside China."[220]

Retaining Global Supremacy

For the United States, there is also the broader objective of retaining global supremacy, on which rests the supremacy of the dollar as
international currency. As Kenneth Rogoff, former chief economist of
the International Monetary Fund, puts it, U.S. "military dominance...
has been one of the linchpins of the dollar."[221] "NATO [the North
Atlantic Treaty Organization] sets its sights on China," reads a recent
Economist headline, reporting that the NATO Secretary General Jens
Stoltenberg wants closer collaboration with Australia, Japan, New
Zealand, and South Korea in order to tackle China's rise.[222] A detailed
report in the same journal explains that this reorientation will address
the problem: "How can the transatlantic alliance hold together as
America becomes less focused on Europe and more immersed in
Asia?"[223] According to a recent study,

> The United States has led NATO to focus on China. Last August,
> NATO Secretary General Jens Stoltenberg stated that "China is
> coming closer" to Europe in the Arctic, Africa, investment in
> critical infrastructure, cyberspace, and investments in modern
> military capabilities. NATO's London Declaration, following
> the December 2019 Leader's Meeting, was the first NATO dec-
> laration to mention China: "We recognize that China's growing
> influence and international policies present both opportunities
> and challenges that we need to address together as an Alliance."
> NATO is conducting an ongoing study, or "analysis exercise,"

related to China that is, according to allied sources, looking into six main issues: cybersecurity; military deployments and Chinese military strategy; Afghanistan; Russia-China relations; Chinese investments in European critical infrastructure and strategic industries; and the impact of China on the rule-based global order.[224]

In March 2019, the European Commission termed China an "economic competitor" and "systemic rival."[225]

The United States and its allies apply pressure on a number of fronts simultaneously, both economic and political. The latest instance is that the United States, United Kingdom, Australia, and Canada have expressed concern over China's imposition of a national security law in Hong Kong (among the personages expressing concern for democracy in Hong Kong, without any sense of irony, was its last colonial governor).

India Positions Itself Against China

It is in this context that India has taken a number of steps in relation to China. As mentioned, Boris Johnson wants India to be part of a group of ten "democracies" ranged, for all practical purposes, against China. Instances of this—such as checks on Chinese investment, the attempt to draw investment away from China, and the promotion of projects/sectors with specific anti-China protection—show how *India's economic stances and policies are becoming more closely entwined with its geopolitical stance.*

Targeting China over COVID-19

India joined U.S.-EU-Australian efforts to target China over COVID-19. This began with the Australian foreign minister demanding a "transparent" global inquiry into the origins of the pandemic, including China's handling of the initial outbreak in Wuhan. U.S. Secretary of Health and Human Services Alex Azar, without naming China, said: "In an apparent attempt to conceal this outbreak, at least one member state made a mockery of their transparency obligations, with tremendous costs for the entire world."[226] India supported an EU-drafted resolution at the World Health Assembly—the World Health Organization's decision-making body—asking for a probe of the organization's response to the coronavirus pandemic, as well as identification of "the zoonotic source" of the coronavirus. Under pressure, China conceded the demand.

On the face of it, who could object to such a probe, with the apparent aim of improving the response to the spread of disease? However, when the United States and its allies press for such sweeping, open-ended exercises, their motives have nothing to do with the purported subject matter and everything to do with strategic military aims with regard to the investigated country. Such were the aims of the unending search for weapons of mass destruction in Iraq, and the investigation of Iran's nuclear program.

Check on Chinese Investment in India

In April 2020, India announced that any foreign direct investment from a country with which it shares land borders would now require government approval. Since Nepal, Bangladesh, Pakistan, Bhutan, and Burma have not been investing in India, the regulation was targeted solely at China. Earlier, foreign direct investment approval had been automatic except in select strategic sectors. The government clarified that this change was in order to curb "*opportunistic takeovers/acquisitions* of Indian companies due to the current COVID-19 pandemic."[227]

The online journal *Swarajya*, which generally voices the Rashtriya Swayamsevak Sangh [Hindu supremacist] viewpoint, clarified that, "as the global slowdown pushes share prices of companies down, China is looking to go on a shopping spree in the season of an induced artificial sale.... It is in the best interests of India to learn from its counterparts in Europe who have been late to realise the economic, social, and political magnitude of Chinese investments in the region."[228]

Since this bar effectively applies only to China, it is clear that opportunistic takeovers/acquisitions of Indian companies by *other* countries, such as the United States, Japan, or the European Union, have the government's approval. There is in fact a pandemic of such opportunistic takeovers of Indian enterprises by (non-Chinese) foreign investors in the wake of India's corporate debt crisis.

Wooing Global Investors Away from China

While portraying Chinese investment in India as a form of "opportunistic takeover," the Indian government has been single-mindedly focused on luring global investors away from China. On April 28, 2020, the prime minister told chief ministers to get their states ready for this task and, on May 1, he held a meeting with top ministerial colleagues to "capture a part of the supply chain that is expected to move out of China as global corporations look to diversify their production base in the aftermath of Covid-19."[229]

According to transport minister Nitin Gadkari, China's weakened global position is a "blessing in disguise" for India to attract more investment. *Bloomberg* reports that India is readying a pool of land twice the size of Luxembourg to offer companies that want to move manufacturing out of China, and has contacted one thousand U.S. multinationals.[230] A paper prepared for the Ministry of Commerce and Industry quivers with anticipation: "Such diversification and shifting of Japanese firms away from China is estimated to create a $730 billion economic opportunity for developing geographies like ASEAN [Association of Southeast Asian Nations] and India. The ongoing COVID-19 crisis presents a golden opportunity for India and Japan to further boost their already successful relationship."[231] (Pursuing "golden opportunities," evidently, is different from being "opportunist.")

For foreign investors planning to invest in industrial production, the availability of cheap or free land, state-of-the-art infrastructure, and a healthy, educated workforce—forms of state subsidies to private capital—are major considerations. They have long enjoyed these in

China. Cheap or free land may be provided by the Indian govern-ment (by ripping it out of the hands of the peasantry), but, given the abysmal state of India's infrastructure and the woeful physical and educational status of its workforce, the Indian rulers' breathless pur-suit of a flood of foreign investment may fall far short of their dreams. (Although significant foreign direct investment has entered in the last few months, it has been "brownfield" investment—that is, the take-over of existing assets, not the creation of fresh ones.)

Nevertheless, this objective is being pursued in all earnest, not only by India, but at the level of the leading imperialist powers as well. David Arase, resident professor of international politics at the Johns Hopkins University Nanjing University Center for Chinese and American Studies, explains: "There is obvious scope for U.S.-Japan cooperation if leaders decide to coordinate their supply chain adjust-ment efforts with Indo-Pacific policy agendas. For example, India is regarded by both the U.S. and Japan as a key strategic and economic Indo-Pacific partner that could benefit from better economic connec-tivity with the advanced West."[232]

Pompeo stated that the Donald Trump administration wants "to mesh the supply chains that both countries [India and the United States] have access to."[233] According to a State Department official, they have "been working on [reducing the reliance of their supply chains in China] over the last few years but [they] are now turbo-charging that initiative."[234]

The United States is pushing to create an alliance of "trusted partners" dubbed the "Economic Prosperity Network," one [State Department] official said. It would include companies and civil society groups operating under the same set of standards on everything from digital business, energy and infrastructure to research, trade, education and commerce, he said.

The U.S. government is working with Australia, India, Japan, New Zealand, South Korea and Vietnam to "move the global economy forward," Secretary of State Mike Pompeo said April 29.

These discussions include "how we restructure...supply chains to prevent something like this from ever happening again," Pompeo said.[235]

Economic Prosperity Network reminds one of the *Greater East Asia Co-Prosperity Sphere*, the term Japan used for the countries it occupied between 1931 and 1945.

Trade Barriers on Chinese Goods

Under the banner of *"Atmanirbhar Bharat"* (self-reliant India), the government now plans to impose higher trade barriers such as licensing requirements or stricter quality checks on 100 products, and additional import duties on around 160 to 200 products.[236] Although the measure purportedly does not target any country, the government has selected commodities such as "wrist watches, wall clocks, ampoules, glass rods and tubes, hair cream, hair shampoos, face powder, eye and lip make up preparations, printing ink, paints and varnishes, and some tobacco items" after a process of collecting information regarding imports from China.[237]

Many more instances could be added to the list of Indian consumer goods and other low technology industries that have been unable to face competition from China. These labor-intensive industries needed protection from cheap imports, Chinese or otherwise, long ago. Some of them have been almost wiped out and it may now take more than tariff protection to revive them. The government's new stance may garner support from small and medium industries in India, which have been bearing the brunt of this competition. Indeed, the Narendra Modi government has always been alive to such political calculations.

However, small and medium industries in India today face a grim future due to the collapse of domestic demand. In the absence of a systematic *plan* for strengthening domestic industry and infrastructure, building a range of domestic capabilities (appropriate know-how, skilled labor, marketing networks, development and use of local resources), and linked crucially to a *widely dispersed increase in domestic demand*, such measures will bring about no generalized improvement in the actual situation of small and medium industries. These trade barriers might only result in the effective reduction in the purchasing power of Indian consumers by making a range of manufactured consumer goods more expensive.

Apart from this, the bulk of imports from China are not low-tech consumer goods, but medium- to high-tech ones, the entry of which the Indian government is not immediately planning to block, for lack of a substitute.

New Policy Stance in Practice: The Case of Adani's Solar Power Project

However, the anti-China policy stance might yield profitable opportunities for favored Indian corporate groups and Western/Japanese multinationals. The latter have in recent years faced stiff competition in India from Chinese firms in high-tech sectors such as telecom equipment, power equipment, and high-speed trains. The Chinese firms' prices are much lower and their quality is said to be comparable, in some cases (such as 5G telecom equipment) even superior.

Take the solar power-related manufacturing sector, where China is overwhelmingly dominant, producing 80 percent of solar cells worldwide and 72 percent of the modules. It enjoys huge economies of scale, with prices dropping substantially every year. India's local photovoltaic manufacturing sector has failed to compete with China, not only on price, but also on quality, and it is almost entirely dependent on China for solar cells. Nor is it alone. While the United States's higher prices are said to be partly compensated by quality, the leading German firm simply wound up its own production in 2013.[238]

The Indian government is now planning to provide import protection for solar-related manufacturing firms based in India, with additional customs duties on solar modules and cells, a guaranteed flow of subsidized power, and financial subsidies (cheap credit and "viability gap funding"—a fancy name for a subsidy given to corporate firms). "Made-in-India solar panels may not be the most competitive.

What may work in India's favor, however, is the strategic shift in the priorities of companies and countries post Covid-19: comparative costs have ceased to be the only criterion for deciding on equipment supply."[239]

This is unlikely to mean self-reliance, however, in the form of Indian firms developing their technological capability to manufacture modules, cells, and other equipment cheaply and well. Rather, it is likely to mean inviting non-Chinese foreign firms to invest here, protecting them from Chinese imports, and providing them subsidies: "India's push could be led by government-owned companies like Bharat Heavy Electricals, which invited international players last month to leverage its 'facilities and capabilities'—16 manufacturing locations, a substantial landbank, and 34,000 employees—to set up base in India."[240]

On June 9, 2020, the Solar Energy Corporation of India awarded the Adani group (one of the corporate groups most closely linked to the present regime) the world's largest solar energy tender: to build eight gigawatts of photovoltaic power plant along with a domestic solar panel manufacturing unit at an investment of ₹450 billion. Adani share prices have doubled since the start of the year.

Such projects are financially impossible for even the officially favored Adani group to execute on its own. Labeled one of India's top ten over-indebted groups in 2012, its debt has since doubled, reaching ₹1.28 trillion by 2019. In the last two years, the group has preferred to borrow offshore, with foreign borrowings now accounting for 30 percent of its debt. Foreign currency bonds in particular doubled from 14 percent of total debt to 25 percent between March 2016 and March 2019.[241] Any sharp depreciation of the rupee should spell trouble for the group, but it leads a charmed existence, seemingly certain that its bets will be winning ones.

The group's growth has been closely linked to government favors and contracts, particularly with the Gujarat government until 2014, and since then the central government. "The group's listed companies saw their value rise by some 85 percent soon after Modi's inauguration, compared to a roughly 15-percent increase for the Sensex over the same period. Within a year of Modi's term at the centre, the companies' market value had risen by over Rs 50,000 crore [₹500 billion]."[242] The Adani group entered solar power in 2013 with a forty-megawatt project in Gujarat and has bet heavily on solar power since then. Winning the latest solar tender is thus not a surprise: "SECI [Solar Energy Corporation of India] enjoys the full support of its 100 percent owner, the government of India," said Adani Green's spokesperson.[243]

As in the rest of the government's "self-reliance" schemes, this exercise may provide profit-making opportunities to (non-Chinese) multinationals, while ensuring that favored corporate groups thrive. Boasting that his group is the only Indian business house with a series of 50:50 ventures with international players such as Total and Wilmar, Adani revealed that he is in discussion with potential equity and strategic partners for solar equipment manufacturing.[244]

The scheme is *directly linked to shutting out China*: Adani claims that, with his solar projects, "the 90 per cent import of Chinese equipment will fall to 50 per cent, and ultimately zero. In 3–5 years, it will be negligible."[245]

In February 2020, Adani hived off several gigawatts of operational solar assets into a new company, with French energy major Total taking a 50 percent stake in the new venture for $510 million—part of the rush of global oil and gas giants into the "renewable" energy market.[246] The Indian government has set a far-fetched target of one hundred gigawatts (one hundred thousand megawatts) of solar power by 2022, but capacity at the end of 2019 was only thirty-six gigawatts. There are big bucks to be made in the sector in the coming years. Adani said Total was "very much interested" in expanding its partnership with Adani Green, as are other foreign investors. The firm's spokesperson said that Adani Green "is always looking for ways to further reduce its costs of capital and to work with other energy majors and traditional investors as a path to facilitating the company's continued rapid growth."[247]

New Policy Stance in Practice: Reliance's 5G

Recent developments in India's telecom sector, too, reflect how the economic policies of India's rulers are now more closely intertwined with their geopolitical stance. They also reveal a closer interlocking of the interests of top Indian corporate firms and foreign capital.

In brief, a leading Indian firm, famous for its proximity to the country's rulers and its influence over regulators, rapidly establishes its hold on the Indian market and abjures Chinese technology in the name of "self-reliance," but in the process opens up rich opportunities for foreign investors from the United States and other developed countries. The newly forged alliance commands unprecedented clout within India.

Reliance Industries Limited, an oil, telecom, and retail conglomerate headed by Asia's richest man, Mukesh Ambani, is India's largest company by revenue, profits, and market capitalization. Since starting operations in 2016, its telecom subsidiary Reliance Jio, armed with huge revenues from privatized oil resources and a range of special, favorable regulatory relaxations, won four hundred million customers and became India's dominant telecom firm.[248] It spent heavily on telecom infrastructure and adopted cutthroat pricing (including free voice and cheap data services for extended periods) to attract customers away from its cash-strapped rivals. Between 2016 and 2019, nine telecom firms ceased operations, either through mergers or bankruptcy, leaving only four, as Reliance Jio snagged top place. The telecom sector wound up with debts of $75 billion, almost three times its revenues, and the telecom market is in danger of becoming a duopoly in the near future.[249]

When Trump visited India in February 2020, Ambani declared at a business roundtable that Jio's 5G network would not have a single Chinese component, to which Trump replied, "well, that's good."[250]

This apparently spontaneous, but carefully choreographed, conversation took place well before the clashes at the Line of Actual Control.

At the time, the Indian government had cleared the participation of Huawei and other Chinese firms in 5G trials in India, and indeed the other major telecom firms in India were planning to use Huawei's technology.

Between April and July, a tsunami of foreign (principally U.S.) investments were made in Reliance Jio. On April 22, the U.S. social media giant Facebook announced that it was investing $5.7 billion in Reliance Jio for a 9.99 percent stake and a seat on the board. This was followed by smaller investments by the U.S. tech giants Qualcomm and Intel, six U.S. private equity firms, and three sovereign wealth funds of Abu Dhabi and Saudi Arabia. Finally, on July 16, Google announced it would be investing $4.5 billion in Jio for a 7.7 percent stake and a seat on the board of directors, apparently in the only global venture it will joins hands with its data-gathering rival Facebook. This brings the total foreign investments in Jio over a three-month period to $20 billion—wiping out Jio's debt of a similar sum. Through these investments, foreign direct investors now own almost 33 percent of Jio.[251]

The combined financial power and data empires of Jio, Facebook, and Google, as well as the depleted financial condition of Jio's rivals, indeed threaten a near-monopoly situation. (Indeed, according to reports, yet another U.S. tech monopoly, Microsoft, is considering joining the bandwagon with a $2 billion investment in Jio.[252] The two firms had recently struck a deal for Jio to use Microsoft's cloud services for businesses.)

At the time of Trump's visit, Ambani did not explain his decision to exclude Chinese vendors, but Pompeo explicitly linked it to U.S. foreign policy when he tweeted on June 24 that "the tide is turning toward trusted 5G vendors and away from Huawei. The world's leading telecom companies—Telefonica, Orange, Jio, Telstra, and many more—are becoming 'Clean Telcos.' They are rejecting doing business with tools of the CCP surveillance state, like Huawei."[253]

Within days of Google's announcement, Ambani stated at the Annual General Meeting of Reliance Industries that Jio "has designed and developed a complete 5G solution from scratch…using 100%

home grown technologies and solutions. . . . I dedicate Jio's 5G solution to our Prime Minister Shri Narendra Modi's highly motivating vision of 'ATMANIRBHAR BHARAT' [self-reliant India]."[254]

According to Jio executives, the firm has been preparing this "solution" for three years, revealing remarkable prescience about the direction of India-China relations. While the media welcomed Reliance's announcement unquestioningly, Ambani's claim mystified informed observers. In its entire existence, Reliance has been known for many things—canny purchases of technology, skilled execution of projects, influence with the regulatory authorities, and ruthless tactics against rivals—but never for the development of technology.[255]

5G technology involves very large investments in research and development over many years, reflected in the over twenty-one thousand patent declarations by eleven firms across the world. The global 5G technology market is dominated by three firms: Huawei, and its smaller rivals Ericsson (Sweden) and Nokia (Finland). These firms bundle the hardware and software into a single package, as well as maintain and upgrade the system. Setting up 5G infrastructure involves very large investments and 5G networks are still under construction in the developed world.

Unlike these firms, which are in the business of telecom technology development and manufacturing, Reliance Jio is a telecom services firm. It started operations just four years ago and has no patents to its name. Jio's 4G was set up entirely, and will be maintained, by Samsung. What then is one to make of Jio's extraordinary claim to having developed a 5G "solution"? V. Sridhar points out that, instead of a full-scale 5G rollout, "patches based on software solutions as well as open source hardware could be built in order to give a '5G-like' network performance, at least in limited markets or geographies."[256]

In such "open platforms," telecom operators opt to buy hardware and software from different vendors. In theory, this could increase competition and reduce costs, but its actual feasibility and performance are far from proved in practice and no developed country has opted for an open-platform 5G as yet.

In its drive to counter Chinese firms, the U.S. government has moved aggressively to take leadership of the groupings that promote such an open structure. The director of the new Open RAN Policy Coalition was until recently a senior official of the U.S. Department of Commerce and the coalition looks to the U.S. government for support.[257]

Whatever the exact contours of Jio's 5G system, it marks an explicit exclusion of Chinese firms and, correspondingly, closer ties with firms of the United States and allied countries. Reliance's principal achievement in telecom has been to capture the market using its financial and political clout. It is now selling shares of this captured entity to foreign investors, in line with the mercantile tendency that has long marked Indian big capital. These foreign firms, which faced some regulatory hurdles in India, will now be handheld by a firm with fabled connections to the rulers.

Data Colonization

Curiously, this operation comes clothed in the rhetoric of nationalism and self-reliance. In January 2019, Ambani called on the prime minister to end "data colonisation" by global corporations:

> Today, we have to collectively launch a new movement against data colonisation.
> In this new world, data is the new oil.
> And data is the new wealth.
> India's data must be controlled and owned by Indian people—and not by corporates, especially global corporations.
> For India to succeed in this data-driven revolution, we will have to migrate the control and ownership of Indian data back to India—in other words, Indian wealth back to every Indian.[258]

By the end of the year, the government introduced a Personal Data Protection Bill in parliament to delineate control over what types of personal data can be transferred outside India. The ostensible ground for the government's ban on fifty-nine Chinese-linked apps on June 29 was that these apps were "stealing and surreptitiously transmitting users' data in an unauthorized manner to servers which have locations outside India. The compilation of these data, its mining and profiling by elements hostile to national security and defence of India…ultimately impinges upon the sovereignty and integrity of India."[259]

The irony is that the business models of Alphabet (parent of Google) and Facebook depend precisely on mining the data of users. As pointed out by John Bellamy Foster and Robert McChesney, "the major means of wealth generation on the Internet and through proprietary platforms such as apps is the surveillance of the population."[260]

Furthermore, major U.S. Internet firms such as Google, Facebook, Microsoft, and Yahoo provide the U.S. government agencies direct access to their users' data, thus forming what has been called a "government-corporate surveillance complex."[261] In turn, "the U.S. government is little short of a private army for the Internet giants as they pursue their global ambitions."[262]

Facebook (including Whatsapp and Instagram) and Google (including Gmail and YouTube) have long been mopping up the data of Indian users. India provides U.S.-based Internet firms free access to its market and has failed to develop strong local substitutes for them (unlike China). But their entry as important investors of India's dominant telecom firm, with directors on the board, in fact marks a further advance in what Ambani had called the "data colonization" of India. This encroachment on India's sovereignty, however, has gone overlooked.

The new Facebook-Google-Jio alliance, armed with huge data about individuals, will have a large impact on a number of sectors of the economy, such as retail trade, online education, health care, and banking. These have vast employment and welfare implications. For example, India's retail trade, composed largely of family-run microenterprises, employs thirty-seven million people. The current lockdowns in India have provided an opportunity for Reliance's new online grocery business, Jio Mart, which was stepped up to two hundred cities in May and is now live on Facebook's Whatsapp.

Jio's "payments bank," a 70:30 joint venture with India's largest bank, the government-owned State Bank of India, began operations in 2018.[263] As in many public-private partnerships, this controversial collaboration implies clear gains for Jio and no clear rationale for the State Bank of India.[264] Google and Facebook both have digital payment platforms, but now may join forces with Jio Payments Bank to create a financial entity with unusual market power in India, taking away business from existing public sector banks.[265]

Political Consolidation

The political implications too are grave. Both Google and Facebook have enormous scope for mass manipulation. Facebook famously conducted at least one manipulative "experiment" on its users without their explicit consent. For a week in 2012, it changed the emotional content of its users' news feeds and found corresponding changes in their emotional expressions.[266] Facebook considered its experiment successful and, indeed, it may have won clients in mass manipulation. Facebook has also explicitly partnered with the Bharatiya Janata Party in its 2014 and 2019 election campaigns. As the former co-convenor of the Bharatiya Janata Party IT cell noted, Facebook and the Bharatiya Janata Party "helped each other."[267] According to Facebook CEO Mark Zuckerberg, "in recent campaigns around the world— from India and Indonesia across Europe to the United States—we've seen the candidate with the largest and most engaged following on Facebook usually wins."[268] Facebook's services to the ruling party were not restricted to the elections. The social media corporation is reported to have denied Congress paid ads to publicize the Rafale controversy and delayed a boost on a *Caravan* exposé on Modi's right-hand man, Amit Shah, by more than eleven days.[269] (As we send this to press, the *Wall Street Journal* has published an investigation documenting the close collaboration of Facebook with the Bharatiya Janata Party regime.[270] Some of these findings were foreshadowed in a series of articles on the website *Newsclick* in 2018.[271])

As for Google, a *Wall Street Journal* investigation recently confirmed that Google had manipulated its search algorithms in order to black-list certain websites for their political views (as well as to favor big businesses over smaller ones).[272] Indeed, Google even provides direct support to U.S. imperialist ventures:

> In 2012, as the civil war in Syria intensified and American sup-port for rebel forces there increased, [Google-owned firm] Jigsaw brainstormed ways it could help push Bashar al-Assad from power. Among them: a tool that visually maps high-level defections from Assad's government, which [Jared] Cohen wanted to beam into Syria as propaganda to give "confidence to the opposition."[273]

The implications of recent investments in India's telecom sector are thus not merely financial. Notably, Ambani is not only the owner of India's dominant telecom company, but also of Network 18, the country's largest media conglomerate, spanning news and entertain-ment in fifteen Indian languages. The entry of Facebook and Google into Jio thus represents an ominous strategic, economic, political, and even cultural consolidation of forces.

Some Caveats

The geopolitical drive against China, led by the United States and drawing in India, advances and intertwines with certain economic interests. It does not signify either that multinationals will withdraw from China overnight, nor that India can discontinue its imports from China, nor that India will be the recipient of all the investment that exits China. (Nor does it signify that, even if India were to receive a flood of foreign direct investment, it would constitute a positive development—but that question needs to be dealt with separately.)

For Western multinationals, China's infrastructure, clustering of firms, scale of production, subsidies, educated workforce, agility in carrying out production changes and delivering on time are in many cases too advantageous to give up quickly. Though China's labor costs have risen, they remain a fraction of those in the United States or even Mexico. Firms from the United States and other developed countries have sunk large investments into China. All this means that a shift from China may take time and may vary from sector to sector.

Nevertheless, holding out to India the prospect of large investments shifting away from China helps orient India more closely to U.S. foreign policy, whether or not much investment finally materializes.

For India, too, an immediate break with trade with China does not appear practical. China was India's largest trading partner from 2013 to 2018. Though the United States appears to have since taken over that position, China remains a very large trade partner. Unlike the United States, which imports more from India than it exports, China runs a large trade surplus with India. To quote Biswajit Dhar and K. S. Chalapati Rao, "India-China trade can be summarised as India supplying raw material and intermediates to China, while importing capital goods and critical intermediates for its pharmaceutical industry, the two-wheeler industry, and for synthetic yarn, among other goods."[274] The extent of dependence on China in several sectors is alarming, such as in active pharmaceutical ingredients. The celebrated Indian pharmaceutical industry restricts itself to making profitable formulations from imported active pharmaceutical ingredients. As such, an interruption in Chinese imports would imperil public health as well as India's exports. Chinese capitalist investments in India are concentrated in the prominent tech sector, in firms such as Ola, Paytm, Zomato, Flipkart, and Byju's. Reportedly, two-thirds of "unicorns"—start-ups valued at $1 billion or more—have Chinese investment.[275]

As such, it would appear that it is much harder for India to disentangle itself from China than for the latter to do without India. Nevertheless, India is clearly taking steps that will set it on a collision course with China.

India Against China: The "Indo-Pacific" Catchphrase

This can be seen most clearly on the level of strategy. In recent years, India has unmistakably become a member of a coalition of powers targeting China. The catchphrase of Indian diplomacy in recent years has been "Indo-Pacific," signifying that India views its strategic interests as extending to at least the South China Sea.

Thus, India's prime minister informed his Japanese counterpart in November 2019 that "India's relationship with Japan is a key component of its vision for peace, prosperity and stability in the Indo-Pacific region." During the visit of India's defense and external affairs ministers to Washington in January 2020, the two sides "reaffirmed their commitment to support 'a free, open and inclusive Indo-Pacific region.'" On June 4, 2020, the prime minister held a virtual summit with the prime minister of Australia and issued a "Shared Vision for Maritime Cooperation in the Indo-Pacific."

It is make-believe to claim that India's security interests stretch up to the Pacific Ocean. It is, rather, the Indian rulers' dreams of great-power status that stretch far beyond India's borders, and far beyond India's material—that is, military and economic—base. The scale of these ambitions is reflected in the writings of the widely published strategic commentator and former member of India's National Security Advisory Board C. Raja Mohan, who views India as the heir of the British Raj:

> The Raj was the principal provider of security in the region stretching from Aden to Malacca and Southern Africa to South China Sea. If the Royal Navy established total dominance over the waters of the Indian Ocean and its approaches, the Indian Army was the sword arm of the Raj in ensuring stability in the vast littoral. . . .
>
> Independent India's opposition to intervention of other powers in its periphery, security assistance to smaller neighbours, and the claim of a security perimeter running from Aden to Malacca are rooted in the definition of territorial India's defence imperatives under the Raj. . . . Like the Raj, India is emerging as one of the important military powers in Asia and the Indian Ocean and *there appears to be new political will in Delhi to see itself as a regional security provider.*[276]

It is of course not India, but the United States, that is heir to the Raj as the hegemon of the region. Nevertheless, it suits the United States that the Indian rulers nurse such notions, since they need India as a junior partner. The current use of *Indo-Pacific* in discussion of diplomatic and strategic affairs in fact originates in the U.S. State Department. Then-U.S. Secretary of State Hillary Clinton

> first used the term "Indo-Pacific" in 2010 to reflect closer naval cooperation with India; "we are expanding our work with the Indian navy in the Pacific, because we understand how important the Indo-Pacific basin is." Whereas U.S. relations with Australia had previously been described and conducted within an "Asia-Pacific" framework, Clinton extended this with "Indo-Pacific" references; "we are also expanding our alliance with Australia from a Pacific partnership to an Indo-Pacific one."[277]

Japan coined the expression *Free and Open Indo-Pacific* in 2016, and Trump embraced the framework in 2017.[278] In 2018, a U.S. State Department official spelled out the reasons for using the term *Indo-Pacific*:

> It's significant that we use this term. Before, people used the term Asia Pacific...but we've adopted this phrase. . . . It is in our interest, the U.S. interest, as well as the interests of the region, that India play an increasingly weighty role in the region. . . . It is a nation that can bookend and anchor the free and open order in the Indo-Pacific region, and it's our policy to ensure that India does play that role.[279]

In May 2018, the U.S. Defense Secretary announced that the U.S. Pacific Command had been renamed the Indo-Pacific Command, "in recognition of the increased connectivity of the Indian and Pacific Oceans."

Why the United States Promotes India's Great-Power Ambitions[280]

Shortly after Clinton introduced the *Indo-Pacific* concept, it was retailed in India by retired top bureaucrats and military men such as former navy chiefs Arun Prakash and Sureesh Mehta, and the influential former Foreign Secretary Shyam Saran (later special envoy for Indo-U.S. civil nuclear issues and chairman of the National Security Advisory Board). Within a few years, it became ubiquitous, with the prime minister, external affairs minister, and foreign secretary adopting it.

The U.S. motivation in promoting the *Indo-Pacific* concept is, in contrast with India's, clear and grounded in reality. A report commissioned by the U.S. Department of Defense in October 2002, titled *The Indo-U.S. Military Relationship: Expectations and Perceptions*, noted that "American military officers are candid in their plans to eventually seek access to Indian bases and military infrastructure. India's strategic location in the center of Asia, astride the frequently traveled SLOCs [Sea Lanes of Communication] linking the Middle East and East Asia, makes India particularly attractive to the U.S. military."[281]

A 2005 U.S. War College study, which draws on discussions its author had with representatives of different military services at the U.S. Pacific Command, states bluntly:

> We need tangible Indian support because our strategic interests and objectives are global, while the military and other means at our disposal to pursue them are not keeping pace.... American force posture remains dangerously thin in the arc—many thousand miles long—between Diego Garcia in the Indian Ocean and Okinawa and Guam in the Pacific.[282]

The Indian public, however, is unaware that their country may be made the linchpin of a broader U.S.-sponsored military alliance for Asia: "during 2003, if not since then, American and Indian officials discussed a possible 'Asian NATO' although *the content of these discussions and of India's significance for them has not been made public.*"[283]

Integrating India into the U.S. Strategic Order

The process of integrating India with U.S. strategic planning was well under way during the United Progressive Alliance government (2004–14), but has proceeded much faster under the Modi government. In 2016, India signed the Logistics Exchange Memorandum of Agreement with the United States, which allows each country to use the other country's specified military installations for certain purposes. (A similar deal was concluded in June 2020, during the virtual summit between Modi and the Australian prime minister.) India has signed other agreements with the United States for secure encrypted communication between the two armed forces and transfer of technology, and is turning increasingly to the United States for military equipment. U.S. arms sales to India rose by more than five times from 2013 to 2017, compared to the previous five years.[284]

The integration of the two militaries is fairly advanced; the two sides have conducted the largest number of joint military exercises between the United States and a non-NATO member. In November 2019, India and the United States held their first joint triservice military exercise (a joint land, air, and sea exercise) in coastal Andhra Pradesh. The United States and Indian navies jointly track Chinese submarines in the Asia-Pacific region. According to one analyst, "the U.S. now accords India almost the same status that it gives NATO member states."[285]

India is also tasked with building ties with a number of countries in the region, including Indonesia, Vietnam, Myanmar, Singapore, and the Philippines. There is little attempt now to conceal the fact that these efforts are targeted at China. Australia may participate in the annual Malabar Exercises in 2020, along with the United States, Japan, and India.[286] The Indian navy recently sailed with the U.S., Japanese, and Philippine navies through disputed waters in the South China Sea.[287] India and Indonesia have concluded an agreement to develop and manage the Sabang port, located close to the strategic Malacca Straits, through which shipping passes to China.[288]

At the political level, India, the United States, Japan, and Australia are the four members of the Quadrilateral Security Dialogue, or Quad for short. At the inception of this process in 2007, China protested that it was a nascent anti-China alliance, and India put it on the back burner. However, since 2017, the Quad has been revived, and in September 2019 the foreign ministers of all four member countries met in New York—a significant escalation. In January 2020, India held a "2+2" meeting with the United States—that is, India's external affairs and defense ministers met their U.S. counterparts, a format the United States reserves for its close allies.[289]

Against India's Interests

However, *none of this makes sense from the angle of India's own security*. On the contrary, it entangles India in distant adventures and threatens to thrust India into wars that serve U.S., not Indian, interests. If India were to pursue its true national interest, it would see through the U.S. intentions of labeling it a "great power," and immediately disengage from these warlike alliances.

Such a clear-headed view of India's national interest would endanger the entire "Indo-Pacific" enterprise of the United States. Only when India sees itself as a great power, a "counterpoise to China in the region," will it want to promote a broad anti-China alliance. And, so, the United States must promote this claim of the Indian rulers. As the U.S. War College study points out,

crucial to making this system work is *India's being convinced of its "manifest destiny" and for it to act forcefully*. It will require in the main that New Delhi think geostrategically and *give up its diffidence when it comes to advancing the country's vital national interests* and its almost knee-jerk bias to appease friends and foes alike. The corrective lies in the Indian government expressly defining its strategic interests and focus and, at a minimum, proceeding expeditiously towards obtaining a nuclear force with a proven and tested thermonuclear and an ICBM [intercontinental ballistic missile] reach. Nothing less will persuade the putative Asian allies that India can be an effective counterpoise to China in the region, or compel respect for India in Washington.[290]

In line with this aim, the United States now terms India a *leading global power.* The U.S. National Security Strategy of 2017 states: "We welcome India's emergence as a leading global power and stronger strategic and defense partner."

Realizing the Goal of "an India Closer to the West"

Seen in this light, the growing hostility between India and China since the emergence of COVID-19, culminating in the clashes between the two armies at the Line of Actual Control, serves the needs of the U.S. grand strategy for the region. With remarkable candor, the *New York Times* greets the recent border clashes with enthusiasm, as the final step in India's journey toward an anti-China alliance with the West:

For years, the United States and its allies have tried to persuade India to become a closer military and economic partner in confronting China's ambitions, painting it as a chance for the world's largest democracy to counterbalance the largest autocracy. This week, the idea of such a confrontation became more real as Indian and Chinese soldiers clashed. . . .

With China facing new scrutiny and criticism over the coronavirus pandemic, Indian officials have recently seemed emboldened, taking steps that made Western diplomats feel that their goal of an India closer to the West was starting to be realized. And some believe the friction with China will push India even further in that direction.

One Western diplomat felt that the coronavirus crisis had made India more eager to build stronger relationships to help it deal with China, and that diplomacy with India was going more smoothly than ever before. "Everyone is more willing, privately, to talk about what to do with China in a post-COVID world," the diplomat said.

Mr. Gokhale, the former Indian foreign secretary, said that countries could no longer ignore Beijing's transgressions and must choose between the United States and China. "In the post-COVID age," he wrote, "enjoying the best of both worlds may no longer be an option."[291]

Truly, COVID-19 has become a useful peg on which to hang agendas that have nothing to do with the health of the people.

8

India's Economy and the Path Ahead

India's economy was in a depression well before COVID-19. Earlier, we described how the period of bubble growth that began around 2003 ended between 2008 and 2010. It was followed by a long downturn. Since then, anxious to please foreign investors (including potential foreign investors in government bonds), the rulers have kept government spending to a minimum, even in the wake of COVID-19. This refusal to spend is both increasing the immediate suffering of the people and deepening the depression of demand. In fact, it is not merely that government spending has failed to increase, but also that—since tax revenues of the central government and the states will collapse this year, and the states' borrowing is severely restricted by the center—the combined spending of the center and states might even shrink.

Having forsworn revival by stepping up government spending, the rulers are instead attempting to revive the economy by promising various incentives to private investors, stimulating their appetites *via* the scrapping of labor laws, provision of cheap and free land, cheap credit, deregulation, privatizations, and so on. However, such measures will not on their own revive private investment, since private investors want to see signs of a demand revival *before* they spend on the creation of fresh productive capacity. Indeed, these measures may further depress workers' incomes, destroy peasant livelihoods, and reduce the meagre social claims of the working people, thereby aggravating the inadequacy of aggregate demand.

The prime minister is also pushing the idea that India can revive growth by integrating further into global supply chains and getting multinationals to leave China and come to India. He terms this, without irony, a policy of "self-reliance."

However, even if some more foreign investment in export-oriented supply chains does come to India as a result of such efforts, it will not lead to sustained growth in employment in India and a revival of India's economy, for a few reasons.

First, foreign investors as a whole are interested not only in exporting from India, but also in getting access to the Indian market itself, where they will displace local producers who are more labor intensive and less import intensive. (At any rate, much of the foreign investment currently taking place is "brownfield," that is, does not create fresh assets, but rather takes over existing firms in order to capture their market shares.) The net effect of further opening up to foreign investment is likely to be reduced employment in India.

Second, in the effort to find India a place in global supply chains, the Indian government is taking steps to keep down wages and peasants' earnings. As noted previously, this will further shrink demand, and thereby economic activity and employment.

Third, global demand is depressed; world trade growth had already collapsed before COVID-19 and, in the wake of COVID-19, is shrinking. Under such conditions, orienting the economy to exports will mean wrestling other third world countries for shares of a shrinking market—a race to the bottom. There is no pot of gold at the end of the global supply chain.

And, so, the outcome of a path of development tied to foreign capital has been:

1. the further foreign takeover of the economy, denationalization of national wealth, destruction of small producers and depression of labor incomes; and
2. the hitching of India to the strategic designs of the global hegemon, thrusting it into harmful military adventures, followed by further military expenditures and internal repression.

This makes it more urgent that India adopt a path of genuine self-reliance and independence, with regard to not only goods and capital flows, but also to political processes.

A Return to Basic Questions

As in the case of all major historical events, the course of the COVID-19 crisis has been shaped by the underlying features of the society in question. Thus, India's grotesque disparities of income and living standards, its seemingly intractable caste system, its gender oppression, and the autocratic nature of the Indian state have all been manifested in the response to COVID-19. We look now at some other underlying features.

Now that growth has slowed down for a decade and turned into a deep depression, it is all the more necessary to return to questions that have been sidelined for forty years, but were the center of study, discussion, and debate among economists in India from the mid–1960s to late '70s: questions such as mass poverty, industrial stagnation due to lack of demand, the structure of demand (emanating from different classes) and its implications for the pattern of industrial growth, the agrarian base of Indian society, and the role of public investment.

Underlying all of these debates was the question of what would play the key role in developing the economy: technological change (linked to infusions of capital) from "above" or social transformation (what was referred to as "institutional change," and the associated changes in who decides the pattern of production and distribution) from "below."

Poverty

For a long time now, we have been told that poverty in India is declining. Indeed, according to the latest figures of the World Bank, a mere 13 percent of India's population was "poor" in 2015, by their definition:

> Since the 2000s, India has made remarkable progress in reducing absolute poverty. Between FY [fiscal year] 2011/12 and 2015, poverty declined from 21.6 to an estimated 13.4 per cent at the international poverty line (2011 PPP [purchasing power parity] $1.90 per person per day), continuing the historical trend of robust reduction in poverty. Aided by robust economic growth, more than 90 million people escaped extreme poverty and improved their living standards during this period.[292]

The World Bank's measures of poverty are bogus, as are those of the Indian government. Neither involves determining whether people actually enjoy the basic necessities of a decent existence. They merely fix an arbitrary cut-off figure in monetary terms and see what percentage of the population falls below it. As a result, vast numbers of people who are actually unable to obtain adequate nutrition, clothing, shelter, medical care, education, transport, and a healthy environment are classified as non-poor. Even if one were to adopt this (wrong) money-metric approach to measuring poverty, the cut-off lines used by the World Bank are set at farcically low levels—no one could survive in the United States on $1.90 a day. An upward revision of the World Bank's line to just $5.50 purchasing power parity per person per day for 2015 (about ₹3,112 per month in that year) would place more than 80 percent of India below the poverty line.[293]

The notion that poverty in India is a marginal phenomenon has now been brutally exposed with the experience of the COVID-19 lockdown. So meagre were the earnings of vast masses of people that, within a month of the lockdown, they had completely exhausted their savings and had money left for only a few days. This has been brought out in survey after survey. Take the Azim Premji University survey, which, although it does not claim to be a representative sample, covers persons from a diverse range of occupations over several states:

> Almost 8 in 10 are eating less food than before. More than 6 in 10 respondents in urban areas did not have enough money for weeks worth of essentials. More than a third of all respondents had taken a loan to cover expenses during the lockdown. More than 8 in 10 respondents did not have money to pay next month's rent.[294]

We quote this not to illustrate the effect of the lockdown, but the conditions of working people *before* the lockdown. The Azim Premji University survey was carried out between April 13 and May 13, 2020—about three to seven weeks after the declaration of the nation-wide lockdown. It took just this short period to render large numbers of people destitute, forced to eat one meal a day in place of two. This tells us that their earnings during *"normal"* times were so low that they were leading a hand-to-mouth existence, with negligible savings.

Similar findings emerge from surveys by numerous other organizations (thirty-three surveys are assembled on the Azim Premji University website).[295] These surveys were largely carried out within about two months of the lockdown. These surveys document the very low earnings of the surveyed persons; their reduced consumption of food; their abstention from all "discretionary" purchases; the exhaustion of their stocks of rations and basic necessities; the exhaustion of their meagre savings (with many reporting having just between ₹100 and 200 in hand); the inability to pay rent, bills, or school fees; growing indebtedness for food; the sale of livestock and tools to meet food needs; the mortgaging and sale of assets (including land); the lack of funds for sowing the *kharif* (summer) crop. Evidently, the savings of working people are insufficient to tide them over for even two months. Any definition of poverty that fails to capture this reality is worthless.

Indeed, the simple fact that 80 to 90 percent of India's employment continues to be in the informal sector, and that half of the employment in even the formal sector is informal (that is, without job security or other benefits), should have alerted any scrupulous analyst to the fact that poverty had not evaporated or merely receded with the efflux of time, but stubbornly persisted. It is a damning indictment of the entire "development process" that has taken place since 1947 and, more particularly in recent decades, the supposed period of high growth.

Stagnation and Recession

Because the reality of mass poverty was universally acknowledged in discussions among economists until the late 1970s, it was possible then to trace the industrial stagnation that had gripped the country since the mid–1960s to the lack of purchasing power among the broad masses. Economists no doubt came forward with very different prescriptions: some urged that, since the Indian market was so poor, production should instead be oriented to export markets; others urged the stepping up of public investment; yet others argued that, unless radical change in agrarian relations took place, the market for industrial goods would remain narrow and distorted. But, at any rate, the contending views all recognized the reality of poverty and stagnation.

Over the course of the next thirty years, the contrary ideas were systematically entrenched by the rulers. First, industrial policy was steadily changed to allow industry to cater to the purchasing power of the elite (later, industrial policy was scrapped altogether). Second, income disparities were allowed, indeed encouraged, to blossom. Third, the economy received periodic injections of foreign capital (earlier as debt, later as investment as well). These combined to fuel sudden spurts of industrial growth, skewed to the elite market, followed by rapid exhaustion of demand and slumps in growth. Each such spurt was then taken as the "new normal" and the succeeding slump was ascribed to "inadequate reform."

The period since 2010 has witnessed plenty of "reform." Yet, industrial growth has *steadily slowed* in this period, finally hitting below zero for the year 2019–20, which included just one week of lockdown. Indeed, if we had a better and more honest measurement of GDP that properly captured the state of the informal sector, where the majority of working people labor, it would show that GDP growth had turned negative for years *before* the lockdown.

It is true that certain ruinous steps by the Modi government, such as demonetization, have depressed demand further. But, essentially, the slowing of growth over a ten-year period cannot be ascribed to this or that action or policy. It is the outcome of a *pattern* of growth. Indeed, the underlying tendency toward stagnation and recession— and not the brief bouts of rapid growth—is the defining feature of India's industrial development.

Now, in the wake of COVID-19, this contradiction—between the drive to revive corporate-led "growth" and the structural constraints of the internal market—is thrown into even bolder relief. The rulers are even more aggressively pursuing "reform" amid a famine of demand by providing a slew of gifts to the corporate sector and foreign investors. Meanwhile, in the economic restructuring process currently under way, the vast army of micro and small firms that account for the overwhelming bulk of industrial employment is being devastated. As such, the present situation underlines the destructive, predatory nature of that accumulation drive, whether or not it brings about "growth" in statistical terms.

Agrarian India

For some time, we have also been told that the importance of the agrarian sphere of Indian society is rapidly fading. After all, agriculture now accounts for just 15 percent of national income, although it still accounts for nearly *half* the workforce. Learned economists tell us that this anomaly needs to be ironed out by ousting one or two hundred million workers from agriculture. The migration of workers from agriculture to cities or other places for work is depicted as a welfare-enhancing free choice, and their earnings in non-agricultural work are described as a subsidy to the agrarian sector.

The lockdown has shattered this notion. It is clear that the vast mass of urban workers have negligible savings from their incomes. They have fled to the villages because they can survive there somehow, even in the absence of wage employment; it is their *refuge*. (Indeed, were it not for this refuge, there may well have been much larger militant upsurges in the urban areas in the wake of the lockdown.) This underlines the role that the agrarian sector continues to play in subsidizing the non-agrarian sector, at the summit of which presides corporate capital. We argued elsewhere that the problem of which sector is subsidizing which depends on how we characterize these households. If we view them as *peasant households*, the inflow of remittances from wage work in urban areas may be perceived as helping a section of peasant families keep their heads above water. But if we view them as *worker households*, it is clear that wages by themselves are far from meeting the consumption costs (what Karl Marx calls costs of reproduction, or necessary labor) of migrant worker households.

Workers' families draw various forms of subsistence from agriculture and common property resources such as forests. The village home serves as a place for cheaply rearing children, vacation and recuperation, and retirement, without which workers would have had to spend heavily on these needs. Tens of millions of workers, such as construction and brick kiln workers, return to their villages during the peak seasons of agricultural work in order to sow or harvest crops on their family plots of land. The harvests from their plots may feed the family for much of the year. So, the portion of consumption met from the agrarian sector helps working-class families keep their heads above water and allows employers to pay the workers less in wages, effectively subsidizing capitalists.[296]

The return of millions of workers to their villages and the likely reduction of urban employment for some time to come imply a larger supply of village labor—indeed, this is already being reflected in employment data collected by the Centre for Monitoring the Indian Economy, as well as in the steep increase in demand for work under the government's rural employment scheme. The sharp drop in demand throughout the country will further depress farmgate prices of agricultural produce, even as input costs rise (due to disrupted supply chains for inputs, as well as the government's increased taxes on diesel), thus worsening the terms of trade for peasants.

These developments may lead to a fall in agricultural wage rates in backward regions (as more workers compete for limited work), an increase in land rents (as more landless peasants try to obtain a subsistence by leasing land), increased rental rates for agricultural machinery, the further narrowing of peasant incomes, and the growth of rural indebtedness due to consumption loans. In brief, India's agrarian crisis is set to worsen.

The lockdown also cast light on certain aspects of India's distorted political economy. Vast underdeveloped hinterlands send forth armies of semi-peasant workers as circular migrants to distant islands of urban growth, and this region-cum-class disparity is continuously reproduced on an ever-larger scale. As millions of workers started crossing incredible distances on foot, no one asked: Why were there no industries near the villages of workers in which they could find employment?

The lockdown and its effects force us once again to consider the central role of the agrarian sector in the process of India's development. Contrary to the view of the ruling classes, the peasantry, landed and landless, who work the agrarian sector are not some troublesome appendages that need to be separated from the land as fast as possible. Rather, to truly develop agriculture means to develop the *productive employment* of the peasantry—and the real development of the country is impossible without this.

This is not fundamentally a technological question, but a social one, of which the question of technology is an integral part. Only if this is done through the conscious democratic mobilization of the vast peasant masses, as part of a broader social transformation, could agricultural growth be organically linked with industrial growth through the development of industry of appropriate scale in rural areas and underdeveloped regions. And only in such a milieu can large industry too play a positive role in relation to the agrarian sector. In an articulated economic structure, both agriculture and industry can play roles as parts of an integrated whole.

The Present System Is a Threat to People's Lives

Another theme of discussion in the late 1970s was the role of public investment; it was felt by some that the stagnation and distortions in the economy since the late 1960s could be traced to the loss of tempo of public investment after the initial phase of planning. Now, the question of public investment has come to the fore in a different way. First, leaving aside driving economic development through public investment, the government refuses to use public expenditure even as a means of reviving demand and stimulating private investment in such desperate times as these. And this refusal is deepening the economic crisis.

Second, the government has been reducing public expenditure on sectors such as public health for three decades now, and this has utterly crippled its ability to address a public health crisis such as the present one.

Indeed, public health and education were sectors that, even in many capitalist countries, received considerable public investment (for example, Britain's earlier National Health Service). These sectors in their heyday were, as it were, small islands of socialism in the sea of capitalism (because the universal right of people to health care irrespective of income is a right that goes against capitalism). These rights were temporarily conceded, in defiance of the laws of capitalism, because of the political challenge from socialist economies at the time. This is underscored by the fact that, with the reversals in socialist countries, those capitalist countries that had earlier conceded these rights as universal have now begun dismantling them.

The COVID-19 crisis has made crystal clear that a private-sector dominated health system is a threat to the lives of people. Most private hospitals, which represent the bulk of hospital capacity in India, withdrew from treating COVID-19 patients, indeed turned them away.[297] Those that have treated COVID-19 patients have charged exorbitant sums, beyond even their steep regular charges.[298]

Remarkably, despite the willful crippling that the public health system in India has had to endure over the past thirty years of "liberalization," and despite the hectic growth of a corporate-led private sector in health, the entire burden of dealing with the pandemic has fallen on the shoulders of the public health system, including its most atrociously underpaid workers.[299]

This makes it all the more necessary to replace the present private sector-dominated health care system with a fully nationalized health care system, over which people have control, with universal, free, and decent health care as a fundamental right. Indeed, it is literally a question of life or death. And, to the extent that such a system is possible only in a different social order, it only makes the struggle for such a social order more urgent.

Imperialism and the Path of Development

In the course of describing India's response to the COVID-19 phenomenon, we have tried to bring out the underlying relationships that shape this response. The financial framework is set by the world's advanced economies, led by the United States. This handful of countries, occupying the summit of global finance, continue to exercise a terrible stranglehold on countries representing the vast majority of the world's population, preventing them from pursuing a course of independent democratic development. The Indian rulers, and the ruling classes who back them, no doubt wield enormous power, indeed hegemony, vis-à-vis the Indian people. But they occupy a subordinate status in the world financial and strategic order, and adhere closely to the rules set by the advanced countries. By doing so, they deliver a steady flow of bounties to the advanced economies at the expense of the Indian people, even in times of grave crisis. India's corporate sector too reaps rich dividends as subordinates within this schema. As strategic rivalries intensify across Asia, the Indian ruling classes have hitched their wagon to the United States and its allies rather than steer an independent course. This may prove ruinous for the Indian people.

What we have been describing are features of *imperialism*, which continues to hold sway over the world. As Harry Magdoff tellingly noted, "polite academic scholars prefer not to use the term 'imperialism,'" but without the concept we are ill equipped to comprehend the reality we confront, or to respond to it appropriately.[300] As imperialism is a system, the response must encompass the system as a whole. Without freeing India from the grip of imperialism, which includes the domestic forces that serve it, the Indian people will not be able to determine their own future or even, as we have seen, save themselves from the direst crisis.

In pursuit of making India a link in global supply chains and competing with other similarly placed countries, India's rulers are obliged to suppress workers' wages and the earnings of peasants. In place of this set up, India must have an alternative path of development. This nation of 1.3 billion must develop its internal market, consisting of workers, peasants, and other working people. For this, it must release them from their many social and economic bondages, as well as radically improve the livelihoods and incomes of oppressed toiling sections—the vast majority of the Indian people. Their demand consists primarily of food and everyday articles of consumption. These can be produced in a widely dispersed way, using technology appropriate *to put the maximum number of hands to work.* At the same time, to garner and deploy its meagre resources, India must put a stop to the grotesque waste and luxury of the Indian elite by divesting them of their assets. When the aim of production is to meet people's basic needs first, rather than to maximize profit, production can be socially planned and not conducted in irreconcilable antagonism with the environment. This does not mean a rejection of large industry, but developing it to complement small industry, promote employment, and conserve the natural environment. Further, if India's aim were to protect its people, rather than aspire to the status of regional satrap of the global hegemon, it can do without spending great sums on arms imports and maintaining bloated armed forces.

All this, the bare rudiments of what we mean by democratic national development, is beyond the scope of India's existing ruling classes.

The Choice Posed Before the People

The present famine of government spending in the face of an unprecedented depression will result in enormous hardship, which in turn
may result in unrest and upsurges. The response so far has been
preemptive, punitive, and severe. As the situation unfolds, the prevailing emergency conditions give scope for the even freer resort to
repressive methods—reliance on security forces, state surveillance,
detention of political activists, heightened communal propaganda,
censorship of independent media, and more—in the name of controlling the pandemic.

These conditions pose more urgently before the people the choice
we have outlined—namely, whether to be resigned to the further
subordination of the Indian economy and its people's lives to global
finance, or take the path of democratic national development.

Notes

1. Himanshu, "The Seriousness of the Problem of Unemployment in India," *Mint*, August 1, 2019.
2. Somesh Jha, "NSO's Consumer Spend Report Showing First Fall in 40 Yrs Won't Be Released," *Business Standard*, February 18, 2020.
3. The differences arise from differing population estimates. Official surveys provide estimates of labor force participation and employment separately for rural men, rural women, urban men, and urban women. These are then applied to population estimates in order to get absolute numbers. The Registrar General of India has stopped issuing figures for the projected population for the years after the 2011 census. The workforce population ratio was 38.6 percent in 2011–12. Himanshu puts the loss of employment between 2011–12 and 2017–18 at 15.5 million (Himanshu, "The Seriousness of the Problem of Unemployment in India"); K. P. Kannan and G. Raveendran put it at 6.1 million (K. P. Kannan and G. Raveendran, "From Jobless to Job-Loss Growth, Gainers and Losers During 2012–18," *Economic and Political Weekly*, November 9, 2019); Santosh Mehrotra and Jajati K. Parida put it at 9.1 million (Santosh Mehrotra and Jajati K. Parida, "India's Employment Crisis: Rising Education Levels and Falling Non-Agricultural Job Growth" [working paper, Centre for Sustainable Employment, Azim Premji University, Bengaluru, India, October 2019.])
4. Mehrotra and Parida, "India's Employment Crisis."
5. S. Subramanian, "What Is Happening to Rural Welfare, Poverty and Inequality in India?," *India Forum*, December 6, 2019.
6. Since 1994, India's agriculture has been opened up to foreign trade and global trends get reflected here. Global agricultural commodity prices

have declined 15 percent between 2008 and 2018, and this trend continued in 2019 (M. Ayhan Kose and Franziska Ohnsorge, *A Decade After the Global Recession: Lessons and Challenges for Emerging and Developing Economies* [Washington DC: World Bank, 2019], figure 1.1.F, 6).

7. Mehrotra and Parida, "India's Employment Crisis." See also "Stagnation in Rural Wage Rates," *Review of Agrarian Studies* 9, no. 1 (January–June 2019).

8. Shalini Nair, "Rural Distress: Last Year of Govt Saw Highest Demand for MNREGA Jobs in 8 Years," *Indian Express*, March 26, 2019.

9. Harikishan Sharma, "As Growth Slows, Demand for Work Under MNREGA Shoots to 9-Year High," *Indian Express*, April 3, 2020.

10. The average consumer price index for agricultural labor rose roughly 8 percent in 2019–20, whereas the average MGNREGS wage per day rose barely 1.7 percent (from ₹179.13 to ₹182.09).

11. Reserve Bank of India, *Monetary Policy Report April 2020* (Mumbai: Reserve Bank of India, 2020), 35, emphasis added.

12. Arnab Dutta, "FMCG Rural Growth Hits 7-Year Low; Poor Consumption Pulls Down Retail Sales," *Business Standard*, October 17, 2019.

13. Sayantan Bera, "New Hunger Games in Jobless Bharat," *Mint*, December 18, 2019.

14. Sayantan Bera, "An SOS from Bharat's poorest citizens," *Mint*, February 3, 2020; *Accidental Deaths & Suicides in India 2019* (New Delhi: National Crime Records Bureau, Ministry of Home Affairs, 2020).

15. Foodgrain Stocking Norms for the Central Pool (Buffer Norms), Department of Food and Public Distribution, Ministry of Consumer Affairs, Food and Public Distribution, Government of India, February 11, 2019.

16. The final installment, with links to the earlier installments, can be found in Ashish Mani Tiwari, "In India's Capital, Fewer Jobs, More Unemployed Workers," *IndiaSpend*, July 10, 2019.

17. Mobis Philipose and Pallavi Pengonda, "Slowdown in Hindustan Unilever's Volume Growth Pre-Lockdown a Big Worry," *Mint*, April 30, 2020.

18. We have used gross value added at basic prices, constant prices. *On Provisional Estimates of Annual National Income 2019–2020 and Quarterly Estimates of Gross Domestic Product for the Fourth Quarter of 2019–2020* (New Delhi: National Statistical Office, Ministry of Statistics and Programme Implementation, Government of India, 2020).

19. Mahesh Vyas, "An Ominous Confluence," Centre for Monitoring Indian Economy Pvt. Ltd., January 14, 2020.

20. Mahesh Vyas, "Financial Investments Trump Fixed Assets," Centre for Monitoring Indian Economy Pvt. Ltd., November 8, 2019.

21. Vyas, "An Ominous Confluence."

22. Kai Schultz and Sameer Yasir, "Unified in Coronavirus Lockdown, India Splinters Over Reopening," *New York Times*, April 28, 2020.

23. Indivjal Dhasmana, "Handling of Lockdown Brings Back DeMo Memories: Economist Jean Dreze," *Business Standard*, March 30, 2020.

24. Mahesh Vyas, "The Jobs Bloodbath of April 2020," Centre for Monitoring Indian Economy Pvt. Ltd., May 5, 2020.

25. Vikas Rawal, Manish Kumar, Ankur Verma, and Jesim Pais, *COVID-19 Lockdown: Impact on Agriculture and Rural Economy* (New Delhi: Society for Social and Economic Research, 2020).

26. Several measures are sheer sleight of hand: formal sector workers are allowed to borrow from their own provident fund accounts; payments scheduled for July under an existing scheme for assistance to farmers (Pradhan Mantri Kisan Samman Nidhi) were to be paid out in April instead; states were instructed to make payments out of an existing fund collected for construction workers' welfare; a long-overdue and appallingly low (₹20 per day) increase in MGNREGA wages was dressed up as COVID-19 relief; the existing District Mineral Fund, which is collected from mining firms and is meant to help the desperately poor communities affected by mining, was to be diverted for COVID-19-related expenditures; women's self-help groups would be able to borrow more, but borrowing has to be repaid, and thus is not a benefit as such; and so on.

27. Amy Kazmin and Jyotsna Singh, "India: The Millions of Working Poor Exposed by Pandemic," *Financial Times*, April 30, 2020.

28. "ILO Monitor: COVID-19 and the World of Work," 2nd ed., International Labour Organization, April 7, 2020.

29. Press Trust of India, "About 400 Million Workers in India May Sink into Poverty: UN Report," *Economic Times*, April 8, 2020.

30. Coronavirus Government Response Tracker, Oxford University; IMF Online Annex Table 1.1: Selected Fiscal Measures in Response to the COVID-19 Pandemic (as of April 8 2020). Fiscal measures here include spending and revenue measures; equity injections, asset purchases, loans, debt assumptions, quasi-fiscal operations, use of extra-budgetary funds; and guarantees on loans and other contingent liabilities.

31. "Government's Economic Package Only 1% of GDP, Say Analysts," *Times of India*, May 20, 2020.

32. Kazmin and Singh, "India: The Millions of Working Poor Exposed by Pandemic," emphasis added.

33. M. Rajeev, "Conditional Enhancement of FRBM Limit Has Little to Offer," *The Hindu*, May 17, 2020.

34. Sandeep Ashar, "Coronavirus Epicentre Maharashtra Freezes All Development Spend for a Year, No New Hiring," *Indian Express*, May 5, 2020.

35. Press Trust of India, "COVID-19: UN Expresses Solidarity with India, WHO Terms Lockdown Comprehensive and Robust," *India Today*, March 25, 2020; Nikhil Agarwal, "WHO Praises PM Modi's 'Timely and Tough' Decision on Corona Lockdown 2.0," *Mint*, April 14, 2020.

36. Suvrat Raju, "India's Lockdown Has Failed. Here's What We Can Learn from It," *The Wire*, May 29, 2020.

37. "In *India*, the fiscal stance should be eased as needed to accommodate necessary increases in public health expenditure in response to the pandemic and shield against a more severe economic downturn, using targeted and temporary measures." *Fiscal Monitor: Policies to Support People During the COVID-19 Pandemic* (Washington DC: International Monetary Fund, 2020), 20.

38. NITI Aayog, *Health System for a New India: Building Blocks—Potential Pathways to Reform* (New Delhi: NITI Aayog, 2019), 44.

39. NITI Aayog, *Health System for a New India*, 44.

40. NITI Aayog, *Health System for a New India*, 172, 174.

41. NITI Aayog, *Health System for a New India*, 175.

42. Amit Sengupta and Vandana Prasad, "Developing a Truly Universal Indian Health System: The Problem of Replacing 'Health for All' with 'Universal Access to Health Care,'" *Social Medicine* 6, no. 2 (June 2011).

43. Sengupta and Prasad, "Developing a Truly Universal Indian Health System," 23.

44. *Key Indicators of Social Consumption in India: Health, NSS 75th Round (July 2017–June 2018)* (New Delhi: National Statistical Office, Ministry of Statistics and Programme Implementation, Government of India, 2019).

45. Mita Choudhury, Jay Dev Dubey, and Bidisha Mondal, "Analyzing Household Expenditure on Health from the 71st Round of Survey by the National Sample Survey Organization in India," National Institute of Public Finance and Policy, July 2019.

46. If we take just the households that actually accessed some form of health care that year, more than half (58 percent) had to make catastrophic payments.

47. "Public Good or Private Wealth? Oxfam Inequality Report: The India Story," Oxfam, 2019.

48. NITI Aayog, *Health System for a New India*, 175.

49. "Public Good or Private Wealth?"

50. Sengupta and Prasad, "Developing a Truly Universal Indian Health System."

51. Sengupta and Prasad, "Developing a Truly Universal Indian Health System."

52. Tilman Tacke and Robert J. Waldmann, "The Relative Efficiency of Public and Private Health Care" (Centre for Economic and International Studies Research Paper 202, Tor Vergata University, Centre for Economic and International Studies, Rome, June 2011)

53. NITI Aayog, *Health System for a New India*, 7.
54. Madhukar Pai, Natasha Correa, Nerges Mistry, and Prabhat Jha, "Reducing Global Tuberculosis Deaths—Time for India to Step Up," *Lancet*, March 25, 2017.
55. Nitin Sethi and Kumar Sambhav Shrivastava, "Govt Knew Lockdown Would Delay, Not Control Pandemic," *Article 14*, April 23, 2020.
56. Nitin Sethi and Kumar Sambhav Shrivastava, "Frustration in National COVID-19 Task Force," *Article 14*, April 24, 2020.
57. "Coronavirus Lockdown: How Modi, Trump Have Responded to the Pandemic," *Indian Express*, March 25, 2020.
58. Sethi and Shrivastava, "Govt Knew Lockdown Would Delay, Not Control Pandemic."
59. Arvind Gunasekar, "COVID-19: Less Than 1% Of 70 Lakh Protective Gear Supplied Domestically," NDTV, April 11, 2020.
60. Raju, "India's Lockdown Has Failed"; Rukmini S., "India Had One of the World's Strictest Lockdowns. Why Are Cases Still Rising?," *Guardian*, July 4, 2020.
61. Order No. 40-3/2020-DM-I(A), Ministry of Home Affairs, Government of India, March 29, 2020; Ditsa Bhattacharya, "COVID-19: Haryana Police to Turn Stadiums into Prisons to Keep Migrant Workers off Streets," *Newsclick*, March 30, 2020.
62. Vikas Rawal and Ankur Verma, *Agricultural Supply Chains During the COVID-19 Lockdown: A Study of Market Arrivals of Seven Key Food Commodities in India* (New Delhi: Society for Social and Economic Research, 2020).
63. "Compilation of COVID19 Lockdown Impact Surveys," in "COVID19: Analysis of Impact and Relief Measures," Azim Premji University, 2020, available at cse.azimpremjiuniversity.edu.in; *COVID-19 Livelihoods Survey: Compilation of Findings* (Bengaluru: Centre for Sustainable Employment, Azim Premji University, 2020); Rahul Lahoti, Amit Basole, Rosa Abraham, Surbhi Kesar, and Paaritosh Nath, "Hunger Grows as India's Lockdown Kills Jobs: Results of a Survey from 12 States," *India Forum*, May 29, 2020.
64. Ashwini Deshpande, "The Covid-19 Pandemic and Lockdown: First Effects on Gender Gaps in Employment and Domestic Work in India" (working paper no. 30, Ashoka University, Department of Economics, June 2020); "How India's Lockdown Has Put Women at a Greater Disadvantage," *Scroll*, April 1, 2020.
65. Anurag Bhargava and Hemant Deepak Shewade, "The Potential Impact of the COVID-19 Response Related Lockdown on TB Incidence and Mortality in India," *Indian Journal of Tuberculosis*, July 10, 2020.
66. Sunil Rajpal, William Joe, **and** S. V. Subramanian, "Living on the Edge? Sensitivity of Child Undernutrition Prevalence to Bodyweight Shocks in the Context of the 2020 National Lockdown Strategy in India," *Journal of Global Health Science* 2, no. 2 (December 2020).

67. Suvojit Bagchi, "India's Next Nightmare: Experts Fear Measles Outbreak As COVID-19 Disrupts Child Immunisation Programme," *Huffington Post*, August 10, 2020.

68. *2020 External Sector Report: Global Imbalances and the COVID-19 Crisis* (Washington DC: International Monetary Fund, 2020).

69. Gaurav Noronha and Deepshikha Sikarwar, "Coronavirus: There's No Free Lunch, Says CEA on Demand for Big-Bang Stimulus," *Economic Times*, May 6, 2020.

70. "Coronavirus Damages India's Growth and Fiscal Outlook," Fitch Ratings, April 27, 2020.

71. Aftab Ahmed and Manoj Kumar, "India Set to Cap Stimulus Package at $60 Billion to Protect Credit Rating, Sources Say," *Reuters*, May 1, 2020, emphasis added.

72. Abhishek Vishnoi, "Markets Will Punish India for Fiscal Excesses, Says Former RBI Governor," *Economic Times*, April 24, 2020.

73. Urjit Patel, "COVID-19 Outbreak Management: A Task Well Begun," *Financial Express*, April 6, 2020, emphasis added.

74. Patel, "COVID-19 Outbreak Management."

75. Raghuram Rajan, "Full Text: Raghuram Rajan on How India Can Get Back to Work After Coronavirus Lockdown," *Scroll*, April 5, 2020.

76. This is in line with what he, as RBI governor, did to the government's control of monetary policy by handing it over to a Monetary Policy Committee.

77. Kristalina Georgieva, "The Great Lockdown: Worst Economic Downturn Since the Great Depression," International Monetary Fund, March 23, 2020.

78. Press Trust of India, "COVID-19: FPIs Pull Out Record Rs 1.1 Trn in March, Highest Withdrawal Ever," Business Standard, April 5, 2020.

79. Nirmal Kumar Chandra, "India's Foreign Exchange Reserves: A Shield of Comfort or an Albatross?," *Economic and Political Weekly* 43, no. 14 (April 2008).

80. In fact, the term *animal spirits* was used by John Maynard Keynes to refer to the state of business confidence: capitalists invest not on the basis of abstract calculations, but when they feel optimistic about making profits. The key element in determining that confidence is the state of *demand*, which is precisely what the present austerity policies are suppressing. The Indian rulers are, however, trying to make up for the abysmal lack of demand by promising capitalists various bounties and the freedom to exploit without hindrance. As such, the term *predator spirits* might be more appropriate in this case.

81. Prime Minister Modi's address to the nation on May 12, 2020. "Full Text of PM Narendra Modi's Speech on Lockdown, Stimulus Package," *Mint*, May 13, 2020.

82. Press Trust of India, "Coronavirus to Have Significant Deflationary Impact Due to Demand Evaporation, Says CEA," *The Hindu*, May 14, 2020.

83. "Karnataka Farmers Protest Against Proposed Amendments in Land Reforms Act," *Newsclick*, August 5, 2020.

84. Radhicka Kapoor, *COVID-19 and the State of India's Labour Market* (New Delhi: Indian Council for Research on International Economic Relations Policy Series no. 18, June 2020)

85. T. N. Ninan, "COVID-19 Is Unravelling the Intolerable Dichotomy of India's Labour Market," *Business Standard*, April 24, 2020.

86. Manju Menon and Kanchi Kohli, "EIA Legitimised Environmental Destruction. Now, Govt 'Renovates' It for the Worst," *The Wire*, June 24, 2020.

87. Tish Sanghera and Disha Shetty, "Environment vs. Economy: An Approach That Exposes India to COVID-19-Like Infections," *IndiaSpend*, May 2, 2020.

88. The research is being carried out by Vijay Ramesh, a PhD student at Columbia University. Jayashree Nandi, "In 6 Years, Forest Land the Size of Nagaland Diverted," *Hindustan Times*, June 30, 2020.

89. Nihar Gokhale, "To Kickstart the Economy, India's Environment Ministry Is Clearing Projects in 10 Minutes," *Quartz*, May 5, 2020.

90. Hannah Ellis-Petersen, "India Plans to Fell Ancient Forest to Create 40 New Coalfields," *Guardian*, August 8, 2020.

91. Thomas Worsdell, Kumar Sambhav Shrivastava, and Ankur Paliwal, "Mapping Land Conflicts and Their Impact on Human Rights and Investments in India," Land Conflict Watch, India, March 2020.

92. Asit Ranjan Mishra, "Modi Invites Foreign Investors, Assures Global Companies of Structural Reforms," *Mint*, July 9, 2020, emphasis added.

93. "PM Modi Seeks US Investment in India's Healthcare Sector," *Pharma Letter*, July 23, 2020.

94. Another reason for expanding the foreign exchange reserves is to prevent the domestic currency from appreciating as foreign capital flows in. This too is a near-compulsory consequence of foreign inflows.

95. The RBI's figure for FPI investment in shares understates the liability by putting it at "historical values"—that is, the sum is actually of the figures that *were* invested over the years. Now, the *current market value* of the shares bought with those figures is multiples of the original numbers. The market value of FPI holdings at the end of December 2019 has been estimated at $463 billion ("India Strategy," Motilal Oswal, May 27, 2020). This is almost three times the figure of $148.9 billion given by the RBI.

96. Official presentations argue that various measures of India's external debt—external debt and GDP, debt service ratio, short term to total external debt, number of months of imports covered by the reserves, and comparisons to peer countries—continue to be comfortable, indicating that the external debt is within manageable limits.

97. Meanwhile, the government may try to prop up the share market by instructing its public sector financial firms to buy shares, thus in

effect reducing the losses of fleeing foreign investors as the latter dump shares. Indeed, that is what happened in March 2020.

98.   The following is a simplified example of what foreign investors fear:

Let us say a foreign fund invests $1 million in the Indian share market at a time when $1 = ₹70. It buys shares for ₹70 million. The share prices rise over time and now the foreign fund's shares are worth ₹80 million.

But, meanwhile, let us say, increased spending by the government has the effect of increasing demand, causing inflation to rise. In other words, the real value of the rupee falls.

As a result, the rupee's exchange rate also falls to $1 = ₹80.

When the foreign fund sells its shares, it gets ₹80 million for them. It converts this back to dollars at ₹80 = $1, and gets exactly $1 million back. It has not made any profit.

Even though this example does not give a correct picture of how inflation happens in India or what actually determines the exchange rate, it does represent what foreign investors fear. Hence, this is one reason why foreign investors press for tight controls on government spending.

99.   Press Trust of India, "Coronavirus to Have Significant Deflationary Impact Due to Demand Evaporation, Says CEA." Government spending can lead to inflation if it causes excess demand, that is, if the economy is working at the peak of its productive strength, without unemployed labor or unutilized industrial capacity. Whereas, in India, even before the COVID-19 crisis, there was broad unemployment and nearly a third of industrial capacity lay idle. Since March, there has been a further collapse of economic activity, employment, and demand for goods.

100.   Parthapratim Pal and Partha Ray, "In Search of a New Theology," *India Forum*, April 3, 2020.

101.   Lucas Chancel and Thomas Piketty, "Indian Income Inequality, 1922–2015: From British Raj to Billionaire Raj?," *Review of Income and Wealth* 65, no. S1 (November 2019). According to Credit Suisse's *Global Wealth Databook 2019*, the top 1 percent in India held 42.5 percent of the country's wealth and the top 5 percent held 63.6 percent. *Global Wealth Databook 2019* (Zurich: Credit Suisse Research Institute, 2019).

102.   "In times like these, the so called 'super rich' have a higher obligation towards ensuring the larger public good. This is for multiple reasons – they enjoy a higher capacity to pay with significantly higher levels of disposable incomes compared with the rest, they have a higher stake in ensuring the economy springs back into action, and their current levels of wealth itself is a product of the social contract between the state and its citizens. Most high-income earners still have the luxury of working from home, and the wealthy can fall back upon their wealth to cope

with the temporary shock." *FORCE 1.0 (Fiscal Options and Response to COIVD-19 Epidemic)* (New Delhi: Indian Revenue Service, 2020), 11.

Therefore, they proposed a moderate, temporary increase in income tax rates for the super-rich or, alternatively, the reintroduction of a tax on their wealth, as well as the reintroduction of an inheritance tax on the wealthy (in developed countries, the rates of inheritance tax are as high as 55 percent). Further, they proposed increased taxes on higher-income foreign companies that have a permanent establishment in India and increased taxes on foreign businesses that earn through advertisement and services (popularly known as the "Google tax," although it would also apply to services such as Netflix, Amazon Prime, and Zoom). "The increased business of these e commerce/ online streaming/ web services companies provides an opportunity to increase the said tax rates by 1%, i.e. from 6% to 7% for ad services, and from 2% to 3% for e commerce" (*FORCE 1.0*, 14).

The government responded to these exceedingly mild proposals with unprecedented alacrity and vindictiveness. Four institutions—the Finance Ministry, the Central Board of Direct Taxes, the Indian Revenue Service Association, and the Income Tax Department—immediately disavowed the report and an inquiry was instituted against the fifty Indian Revenue Service officers associated with the report (Prabhjote Gill, "No Tax on India's Super-Rich – Government Issues an Inquiry Against 50 IRS Officers Who Released the 'FORCE' Report," *Business Insider*, April 27, 2020). According to sources in the Finance Ministry, this effort was an act of "indiscipline," as "the government is doing its best to provide relief and liquidity into the system and ease the lives of people in these trying times" (Dipak Mondal, "Govt Calls Rogue IRS Panel's Super Rich Tax Proposals 'Irresponsible,'" *Business Today*, April 26, 2020).

103. Dipak Mondal, "Chargesheets Against 3 IRS Officers for Report Suggesting Super-Rich Tax," *Business Today*, April 27, 2020.

104. R. Nagaraj, "India's Dream Run, 2003–08: Understanding the Boom and Its Aftermath," *Economic and Political Weekly* 48, no. 20 (May 2013).

105. As inflows take place and the supply of dollars increases in the foreign exchange market, the rupee's value tends to rise. This would have a harmful impact on Indian producers, since imported goods would become cheaper in rupees and Indian exports would become more expensive in dollars. Hence, in response to a rise in inflows, the Reserve Bank intervenes to buy up the dollars, which it adds to its foreign exchange reserves. In exchange for these dollars, the RBI pays rupees, which end up in the banks. As a result, banks have additional funds with which to lend and are under pressure to lend. See C. P. Chandrasekhar, "Missing the Big Picture: Arvind Subramanian

and Josh Felman on the 'Great Slowdown,'" International Development Economics Associates, December 22, 2019.

106. The higher share prices rise, the heftier the premium (over the face value of the share) companies can charge when raising money from the public through fresh share issues.

107. *Economic Survey 2016–17* (New Delhi: Government of India, Ministry of Finance, Department of Economic Affairs, Economic Division, 2017), 86.

108. K. C. Chakrabarty, "Infrastructure Financing by Banks in India: Myths and Realities," *RBI Monthly Bulletin*, September 2013, 68–69.

109. Gajendra Haldea, "Sub-Prime Infrastructure: Crony Capitalism in Public Sector Banks" (discussion paper, New Delhi, August 2015), 3–4.

110. *Report of the Expert Committee to Revise and Strengthen the Monetary Policy Framework* (Mumbai: Reserve Bank of India, 2014), 21, emphasis added.

111. Although much of this "success" can be explained by the fall in international oil prices, this was no achievement of the government.

112. *Economic Survey 2014–15*, vol. 1 (New Delhi: Government of India, Ministry of Finance, Department of Economic Affairs, Economic Division, 2015), 70–72, emphasis added.

113. *Economic Survey 2016–17*, 86–87.

114. *Economic Survey 2016–17*, 88–91, emphasis added.

115. Deblina Saha, "PPPs in India – Will They Regain Their Former Glory?," World Bank blogs, July 4, 2017; *Private Participation in Infrastructure: 2019 Annual Report* (Washington DC: World Bank, 2019).

116. V. Narayanan, "India Inc Increasingly Looks Abroad for Funds," *Hindu Business Line*, October 8, 2019.

117. Radhika Pandey and Amrita Pillai, "COVID-19 and the MSME Sector: The 'Identification' Problem," Ideas for India, April 20, 2020.

118. *Key Indicators of Unincorporated Non-Agricultural Enterprises (Excluding Construction) in India, NSS 73rd Round (July 2015–June 2016)* (New Delhi: National Sample Survey Office, Ministry of Statistics and Programme Implementation, Government of India, 2017).

119. Data for the informal sector is collected in sample surveys at intervals of several years. In the interim, estimates for informal sector output are made based on the relationship between the formal and informal sectors at the time of the last survey. However, during certain crises, the informal sector is affected much more than the formal sector. Indeed, the latter may even benefit as the former shrinks. Yet, GDP calculations continue to be made as if the earlier relationship still held. Akshay Deshmane, "Indian Economy in Recession Thanks to Demonetisation, Says Economist Arun Kumar," *Huffington Post*, November 13, 2019.

120. *Report of the Expert Committee on Micro, Small and Medium Enterprises*

(Mumbai: Reserve Bank of India, 2019). Even 40 percent appears to be an overestimate.

121. Pandey and Pillai, "COVID-19 and the MSME Sector."

122. Namrata Acharya, "MSMEs Forced to Approach Moneylenders as PSBs Steer Clear Despite Government Push," *Business Standard*, May 6, 2019.

123. *Report of the Expert Committee on Micro, Small and Medium Enterprises*, 22.

124. "Unpaid Dues to MSME Sector May Be Over Rs 5 Lakh Crore, Says Gadkari," *The Wire*, May 15, 2020.

125. Procurement by central public sector enterprises from MSMEs in 2017–18 was less than ₹250 billion (*Report of the Expert Committee on Micro, Small and Medium Enterprises*).

126. Vyas, "An Ominous Confluence," emphasis added.

127. Namrata Acharya, "MSMEs Forced to Approach Moneylenders as PSBs Steer Clear Despite Government Push."

128. Rathin Roy, "A Silent Fiscal Crisis?," *Business Standard*, July 6, 2019.

129. V. Sridhar, "Dystopian Pipe Dream," *Frontline*, May 22, 2020.

130. Sridhar, "Dystopian Pipe Dream."

131. As Mahesh Vyas points out, India's labor force participation rate—the percentage either employed or seeking work—is about a third less than the global average of 66 percent. Employment levels are less than 40 percent. Mahesh Vyas, "Surveying India's Unemployment Numbers," *The Hindu*, February 9, 2019.

132. "India's International Investment Position (IIP), December 2019," Reserve Bank of India, March 31, 2020; "India Strategy," Motilal Oswal.

133. Peeyush Dalmia, Vivek Pandit, Gaurav Sharma, and Dushyant Singh, *Indian Private Equity: Coming of Age* (New York: McKinsey & Company, 2018).

134. Surajeet Das Gupta and Sachin Mampatta, "Foreign Investors Picking Controlling Stakes in Companies on the Rise," *Business Standard*, June 8, 2019.

135. Vikram Utamsingh, Nandini Chopra, Nikhil Shah, and Harkamal Ghuman, *India's M&A and Distressed Opportunity Landscape* (Mumbai: Alvarez & Marsal, 2019).

136. Nagaraj, "India's Dream Run, 2003–08."

137. Andy Mukherjee, "Private Equity Spies Profit in India's Distress," *Bloomberg*, November 7, 2019.

138. Ridhima Saxena, "PE Funds Increasingly Look for Buyout Deals in India," *Mint*, May 12, 2019.

139. Lalatendu Mishra, "Foreign Funds 'Take Over' Indian Road Assets," *The Hindu*, September 18, 2019.

140. Tanya Thomas, "The Great Games at Play in Wind and Solar," *Mint*, July 14, 2020.

141. Thomas, "The Great Games at Play in Wind and Solar."
142. Mukherjee, "Private Equity Spies Profit in India's Distress," emphasis added.
143. Utamsingh, Chopra, Shah, and Ghuman, *India's M&A and Distressed Opportunity Landscape.*
144. M. Rajshekhar, "Crony Capitalism on Modi's Watch Means Invisible Hands Ensure You Never Go Bankrupt," *The Wire*, July 29, 2020.
145. Pallavi Pengonda and Mobis Philipose, "Why Has Rosneft Paid a Packet for Essar Oil?," *Mint*, October 18, 2016.
146. Rajshekhar, "Crony Capitalism on Modi's Watch Means Invisible Hands Ensure You Never Go Bankrupt."
147. M. Rajshekhar, "India's Bid to Fix Bad Loan Crisis Is Reshaping Its Corporate Sector – and Creating New Challenges," *Scroll*, October 31, 2018.
148. Rahul Varman, "Royalty Payments: The Royal Treatment of Foreign Companies in India," Research Unit for Political Economy (blog), March 9, 2014, available at rupeindia.wordpress.com.
149. Anto Antony, "Reliance to Offer $20 Bn Stake in Retail Business to Amazon: Report," *Bloomberg*, September 10, 2020.
150. Arindam Majumder, "Adani Group Acquires 74 Percent Stake in Mumbai International Airport", *Business Standard*, September 1, 2020.
151. Dinesh Khanna, Jason LaBresh, Jens Kengelbach, Daniel Selikowitz, James Argent, and Emily Burke, "The $75 Trillion Opportunity in Public Assets," Boston Consulting Group, October 18, 2018, emphasis in the original. Regarding their role as advisors to the Indian government on COVID-19, Boston Consulting Group admits: "We don't claim we are epidemiologists. But we certainly know what crisis reforms should be."
152. LexOrbis, "The Government of India's Tryst with Privatisation," *Lexology*, June 1, 2020, emphasis in the original.
153. Twesh Mishra, "Survey Moots a Holding Company to Vest Govt's Stake in CPSEs," *Business Line*, January 31, 2020, emphasis added
154. Pallavi Pengonda, "With Interest Already High, Govt Should Make Most of BPCL Sale," *Mint*, December 2, 2019.
155. Rounak Jain, "India May Have to Sell BPCL Shares for Less Than the Best Price as the Government Needs Money," *Business Insider*, May 28, 2020.
156. Pengonda, "With Interest Already High, Govt Should Make Most of BPCL Sale."
157. C. P. Chandrashekhar, "Reliance and Facebook: Seeking Pathways to Profit," International Development Economics Associates, May 7, 2020. The Canadian private equity fund Brookfield bought the Reliance Industries-owned East West Pipeline for ₹130 billion in 2019. Shine Jacob, "Brookfield to Acquire Mukesh Ambani's East-West Pipeline for Rs 13,000 Cr," *Business Standard*, March 15, 2019.
158. James Crotty and Kang-Kook Lee, "Was the IMF's Imposition of

Economic Regime Change in Korea Justified? A Critique of the IMF's Economic and Political Role in Korean During and After the Crisis," *Review of Radical Political Economics* 41, no. 2 (2009).

159. Jomo K. S., "East Asia: From Miracle to Debacle and Beyond?," 2002, available at networkideas.org.

160. Crotty and Lee, "Was the IMF's Imposition of Economic Regime Change in Korea Justified?"

161. Crotty and Lee, "Was the IMF's Imposition of Economic Regime Change in Korea Justified?"

162. Kang-Kook Lee, "Neoliberalism, the Financial Crisis, and Economic Restructuring in Korea," in *New Millennium South Korea: Neoliberal Capitalism and Transnational Movements*, ed. Jesook Song (New York: Routledge, 2011), 36–38.

163. Lee, "Neoliberalism, the Financial Crisis, and Economic Restructuring in Korea."

164. Lee, "Neoliberalism, the Financial Crisis, and Economic Restructuring in Korea."

165. Lee, "Neoliberalism, the Financial Crisis, and Economic Restructuring in Korea."

166. Crotty and Lee, "Was the IMF's Imposition of Economic Regime Change in Korea Justified?"

167. Jacques-chai Chomthongdi, "The IMF's Asian Legacy," Global Policy Forum, September 2000.

168. Letter from Kyung-Shik Lee and Chang-Yuel Lim to Michel Camdessus, February 7, 1998.

169. Kwang-Yeong Shin, "Globalisation and the Working Class in South Korea: Contestation, Fragmentation and Renewal," *Journal of Contemporary Asia* 40, no. 2 (May 2010): 222.

170. Akira Suehiro, "Family Business Gone Wrong? Ownership Patterns and Corporate Performance in Thailand," (Asian Development Bank Institute Working Paper Series no. 19, Tokyo, May 2001).

171. Suehiro, "Family Business Gone Wrong?"

172. Labros S. Skartsis, https://www.academia.edu/6655991/Media_Coverage _of_the_2010_Greek_Debt_Crisis_Inaccuracies_and_Evidence_of_ Manipulation.," Academia, 2014.

173. "Greece: Request for Stand-By Arrangement," International Monetary Fund, May 2010.

174. Costas Lapavitsas, "Political Economy of the Greek Crisis," *Review of Radical Political Economics* 51, no. 1 (2019).

175. Lapavitsas, "Political Economy of the Greek Crisis."

176. "Greece: Request for Stand-By Arrangement."

177. Barry Eichengreen et al., *Independent Report on the Greek Official Debt* (London: Centre for Economic Policy Research, Policy Insight no. 92, 2018).

178. *Greece: Staff Report for the 2019 Article IV Consultation* (Washington DC: International Monetary Fund, 2019).

179. Greece's crisis came at a fortuitous time for advanced economies such as the United States, United Kingdom, Germany, and Japan, which had embarked on large government borrowing programs to revive their economies in the wake of the Great Financial Crisis. When the panic emerged in 2010 over the Greek public debt, international financial investors began selling off their Greek government bonds. They sought to shift their investments to "safe havens"—the government bonds of countries that would never default, strong economies such as the four just listed. This "flight to safety" meant that, with many investors rushing to buy government debt of strong economies, the effective interest rate on such government debt fell, even as the interest rate on Greek government bonds soared. As a result, the strong economies enjoyed vast savings on their government borrowings.

A study noted: "Any time there was bad news about Greece, yields [effective interest rates] on German government bonds fell, and any time there was good news about Greece, German government bond yields rose.... the savings of the German budget are estimated to be more than € 100 billion (or in excess of 3 per cent of GDP) during the course of 2010 to 2015.... By most accounts, Germany's share in the bailout package... amounts to no more than € 90 billion.... Hence, in case Greece defaults on its debts... the maximal uncertain and future costs of bailing out Greece to Germany are smaller than the benefits already accrued to the German budget." Reint E. Gropp, "Germany Benefited Substantially from the Greek Crisis," Halle Institute for Economic Research, August 10, 2015. See also Skartsis, "Media Coverage of the 2010 Greek Debt Crisis."

180. A primary budget surplus is government revenues minus government expenditure (*excluding* interest payments); Eichengreen et al., *Independent Report on the Greek Official Debt.*

181. "Greece: Request for Stand-By Arrangement."

182. "Six Key Points About Greek Debt and the Forthcoming Election," Jubilee Debt Campaign, January 2015.

183. "Six Key Points About Greek Debt and the Forthcoming Election."

184. Olivier Blanchard and Daniel Leigh, "Growth Forecast Errors and Fiscal Multipliers" (International Monetary Fund Working Paper 13/1, January 2013).

185. "Greece: Selected Issues" (International Monetary Fund Country Report no. 19/341, International Monetary Fund, November 2019), 4.

186. *Greece: Staff Report for the 2019 Article IV Consultation*, 13.

187. *OECD Economic Surveys: Greece 2018* (Paris: Organisation for Economic Co-operation and Development, 2018).

188. "Multidimensional Poverty Headcount Ratio (% of Total Population) – Greece," World Bank, accessed September 23, 2020.

189. "Delayed Greek Asset Sales Pick Up Steam as Bail-Out Approaches End," *Financial Times*, June 5, 2018.

190. Verena Nees, "Television Programme Shows How German Companies Benefit from Privatisation Programme in Greece," World Socialist Website, July 30, 2015.

191. *Greece: Staff Report for the 2019 Article IV Consultation*, 58.

192. Eleni Portaliou, "Greece: A Country for Sale," *Jacobin*, September 12, 2016.

193. Lapavitsas, "Political Economy of the Greek Crisis."

194. Portaliou, "Greece."

195. "2019 Investment Climate Statements: Greece," U.S. Department of State, 2019, available at state.gov.

196. Portaliou, "Greece."

197. Press Trust of India, "Govt to Start Raising Part of Its Gross Borrowings from External Markets: FM," *Outlook*, July 5, 2019.

198. "Michael R. Bloomberg and Indian Prime Minister Narendra Modi Announce Partnership to Strengthen Global Investment in India," *Bloomberg*, September 25, 2019.

199. Usually, the measure used is market capitalization: the number of bonds times the price of the bond.

200. Urjit Patel, "A Task Well-Begun and What Needs to be Done," *Indian Express*, April 6, 2020, emphasis added.

201. C. P. Chandrashekhar, "Angling for a Swap Line," *Frontline*, May 8, 2020.

202. Urjit Patel, "Financial Regulations and Economic Policies for Avoiding the Next Crisis" (lecture, 32nd Annual G30 International Banking Seminar, Inter-American Development Bank, Washington DC, October 15, 2017), 5–7.

203. *The Covid-19 Shock to Developing Countries: Towards a "Whatever It Takes" Programme for the Two-Thirds of the World's Population Being Left Behind* (Geneva: United Nations Conference on Trade and Development, 2020), 9.

204. Kose and Ohnsorge, *A Decade After the Global Recession*, 16.

205. Matthew P. Goodman, Stephanie Segal, and Mark Sobel, "Assessing the G20 Virtual Summit," Center for Strategic and International Studies, March 27, 2020.

206. C. P. Chandrashekhar and Jayati Ghosh, "When the US and India Together Failed the Developing World," *Business Line*, April 21, 2020; Jayati Ghosh, "Why India Should Support an SDR Issue by the International Monetary Fund", *The Wire*, April 17, 2020.

207. "Pompeo: China's Behaviour Was Unacceptable in Its Border Clash with India," *DD News*, July 23, 2020.

208. Sriram Lakshman, "U.S. Secretary of State Pompeo Welcomes India's Chinese App Ban," *The Hindu*, July 2, 2020.

209. Mercy Kuo, interview with David Arase, "Japan Prods Firms to Leave

China, Affecting Ties with Beijing and Washington," *Diplomat*, May 8, 2020.

210. "As China Pushes Back on Virus, Europe Wakes to 'Wolf Warrior' Diplomacy," *Reuters*, May 14, 2020.

211. "Coronavirus: Macron Questions China's Handling of Outbreak," *BBC*, April 17, 2020.

212. Silvia Amaro, "EU Chief Backs Investigation into Coronavirus Origin and Says China Should Be Involved," *CNBC*, May 1, 2020.

213. Steven Erlanger, "Global Backlash Builds Against China Over Coronavirus," *New York Times*, May 3, 2020.

214. "Multinational Companies Are Adjusting to Shorter Supply Chains," *Economist*, July 11, 2019.

215. "Multinational Companies Are Adjusting to Shorter Supply Chains."

216. "Companies Must Get Ready for a Riskier World," *Economist*, July 11, 2019.

217. Nikita Kwatra, "Why Falling for Anti- China Mood Could Hurt Trade," *Mint*, June 4, 2020.

218. Natasha Lomas, "UK U-Turns on Huawei and 5G, Giving Operators Until 2027 to Rip Out Existing Kit," *Tech- Crunch*, July 14, 2020.

219. Lucy Fisher, "Downing Street Plans New 5G Club of Democracies," *Times*, May 29, 2020.

220. "Companies Must Get Ready for a Riskier World."

221. Kenneth Rogoff, "America Will Need $1,000 Billion Bail-Out," *Financial Times*, September 17, 2008.

222. "NATO Sets Its Sights on China," *Economist*, June 9, 2020.

223. "How NATO Is Shaping Up at 70," *Economist*, March 19, 2019.

224. Andrés Ortega Klein, "The U.S.-China Race and the Fate of Transatlantic Relations, Part II: Bridging Differing Geopolitical Views," Center for Strategic and International Studies, April 23, 2020.

225. *EU-China—A Strategic Outlook* (Brussels: European Commission, 2019).

226. Shubhajit Roy, "WHO Nod for Coronavirus Probe, China Backs Down," *Indian Express*, May 19, 2020.

227. Sunanda Sen, "New FDI Norms in Time of COVID—Good Economics or Geopolitics?," *The Wire*, May 2, 2020, emphasis added.

228. Tushar Gupta, "Restricting Chinese FDI into India: How China Uses Financial Crisis to Further Its Expansionist Agenda," *Swarajya*, June 18, 2020.

229. "Covid-19: PM Modi Signals Push to Attract Firms That Exit China to India," *Times of India*, May 1, 2020.

230. Nikhil Inamdar, "Coronavirus: Can India Replace China as World's Factory?," *BBC*, May 18, 2020.

231. IANS, "India Pitches for Japanese Companies as They Move Out of China," *Outlook*, May 13, 2020.

232. Kuo, interview with Arase, "Japan Prods Firms to Leave China, Affecting Ties with Beijing and Washington."

233. Indrani Bagchi, "US, India Working Jointly on Covid Vaccine: Pompeo," *Times of India*, April 17, 2020.

234. "Trump Administration Pushing to Rip Global Supply Chains from China: Officials," *Reuters*, May 4, 2020.

235. "Trump Administration Pushing to Rip Global Supply Chains from China."

236. "India Plans Higher Trade Barriers, Raised Import Duties on 300 Foreign Products: Report," *Reuters*, June 18, 2020.

237. "Amid Border Tension, PMO Seeks Product-Wise Details from India Inc to Curb China Imports," *News18*, June 21, 2020.

238. Christoph K. Klunker, "Let China Pay for India's Solar Push," *Mint*, August 9, 2018.

239. Vandana Gombar, "Taking on China in Solar Manufacturing," *Business Standard*, June 9, 2020.

240. Gombar, "Taking on China in Solar Manufacturing."

241. Aman Kapadia and Forum Bhatt, "Adani Group's Growing Debt Pile Is Changing Colour," *Bloomberg Quint*, November 5, 2019.

242. Nileena MS, "The Massive Indebtedness of the Adani Group and Its Convenient Relations with Government Enterprises," *Caravan*, March 15, 2018.

243. John Parnell, "India's Adani Wins World's Largest Solar Tender," *Green Tech Media*, June 10, 2020.

244. "Solar Equipment Imports from China Will Fall to Zero in 3–5 Years, Says Gautam Adani," ET Now Digital, June 10, 2020.

245. "Solar Equipment Imports from China Will Fall to Zero in 3–5 Years, Says Gautam Adani."

246. John Parnell, "Total and Shell Give Green Lights to Big Solar Investments in India and Australia," *Green Tech Media*, February 6, 2020.

247. Parnell, "India's Adani Wins World's Largest Solar Tender."

248. Kiran Stacey and Simon Mundy, "India: The Creation of a Mobile Phone Juggernaut," *Financial Times*, January 10, 2018.

249. Daniel Block, "Data Plans: How Government Decisions Are Allowing Reliance Jio to Monopolise the Telecom Sector," *Caravan*, February 1, 2019.

250. "Remarks by President Trump at a Business Roundtable | New Delhi, India," White House, February 26, 2020.

251. This is apart from foreign portfolio investors' holdings of about one-fourth of the equity of the parent company, Reliance Industries Limited, which holds the remaining 67 percent of Jio.

252. Anirudh Laskar and Swaraj Singh Dhanjal, "Now, Microsoft Eyes Stake in Jio," *Hindustan Times*, May 27, 2020.

253. Tweet, posted by Secretary Pompeo (@SecPompeo), June 24, 2020.

254. "RIL AGM 2020: Read the Full Text of Mukesh Ambani's Speech," *Money Control*, July 16, 2020, emphasis in the original.

255. In the past, loud official claims of building up domestic enterprise have often gone hand in hand with the undermining of domestic manufacturing and the deepening of import dependence. When Modi announced the "Make in India" campaign in 2014, he claimed it would make India into a global manufacturing hub. Among the targets was the domestic manufacture of mobile phones in India, for which India is one of the world's largest markets. Indeed, in an apparent success for the campaign, India has now become the second-largest mobile phone manufacturer in the world, after China. However, as Sunil Mani brings out in a recent devastating study, all that has taken place is local assembly of imports by multinational firms and, in the process, import dependence has actually *deepened*. Value added as a share of the value of output has declined sharply and the outflow on account of royalty, license fees, and repatriation of profits has increased sharply. See Sunil Mani, "Developing India's Mobile Phone Manufacturing Industry," *Economic and Political Weekly* 55, no. 19 (May 2020).

256. V. Sridhar, "Reliance's 5G Claims Are Short on Substance," *Frontline*, July 18, 2020. Prabir Purkayastha points out that the U.S. firm Qualcomm, one of the recent investors in Jio, is also a significant developer of 5G technology and may play a role in Reliance's 5G-lite "solution" (personal communication).

257. Alan Weissberger, "Open RAN Policy Coalition: U.S. Attempt to Exclude Chinese 5G Network Equipment Vendors?," *Tech Blog*, May 5, 2020.

258. "Read the Full Text of Mukesh Ambani's Speech at Vibrant Gujarat Summit 2019," *CNBC*, January 18, 2019.

259. "Government Bans 59 Mobile Apps Which Are Prejudicial to Sovereignty and Integrity of India, Defence of India, Security of State and Public Order," Ministry of Electronics and IT, June 29, 2020, available at pib.gov.in.

260. John Bellamy Foster and Robert W. McChesney, "Surveillance Capitalism: Monopoly-Finance Capital, the Military-Industrial Complex, and the Digital Age," *Monthly Review* 66, no. 3 (July–August 2014).

261. Foster and McChesney, "Surveillance Capitalism." The phrase was coined by Beatrice Edwards of the Government Accountability Project.

262. Foster and McChesney, "Surveillance Capitalism."

263. A special type of bank in India that can accept deposits and make payments but cannot extend credit.

264. Abir Dasgupta and Paranjoy Guha Thakurta, "Jio Payments Bank and SBI: A Camel Inside a Tent?," *Newsclick*, July 2, 2020.

265. Prabir Purkayastha, "From Atmanirbhar to Reliance India," *Newsclick*, July 27, 2020.

266. Adam D. I. Kramer, Jamie E. Guillory, and Jeffrey T. Hancock, "Experimental Evidence of Massive-Scale Emotional Contagion Through Social Networks," *Proceedings of the National Academy of the Sciences of the United States of America* 111, no. 24 (June 2014).

267. Partha P. Chakrabartty, "The Past and Future of Facebook and BJP's Mutually Beneficial Relationship," *The Wire*, June 3, 2019.

268. "Here Is What Mark Zuckerberg Said About PM Modi in a Facebook Post," *Hindustan Times*, February 17, 2017.

269. Chakrabartty, "The Past and Future of Facebook and BJP's Mutually Beneficial Relationship."

270. Newley Purnell and Jeff Horwitz, "Facebook's Hate-Speech Rules Collide with Indian Politics," *Wall Street Journal*, August 14, 2020.

271. Cyril Sam and Paranjoy Guha Thakurta, "Is Facebook in India Truly Independent of Political Influence? Not Really – It Has Backed Modi and BJP," *Newsclick*, November 22, 2018. This was followed by another four articles on the same website between November 23 and 26, 2018.

272. Kirsten Grind, Sam Schechner, Robert McMillan, and John West, "How Google Interferes with Its Search Algorithms and Changes Your Results," *Wall Street Journal*, November 15, 2019; Andre Damon, "Wall Street Journal Investigation Confirms Google Operates Censorship Blacklist," World Socialist Web Site, November 18, 2019.

273. Yasha Levine, "Google's Earth: How the Tech Giant Is Helping the State Spy on Us," *Guardian*, December 20, 2018.

274. Biswajit Dhar and K. S. Chalapati Rao, "India's Economic Dependence on China," *India Forum*, August 7, 2020.

275. Zia Haq, "From Infrastructure to Hi-Tech: Mapping China's Large Trade Footprint in India," *Hindustan Times*, June 19, 2020.

276. C. Raja Mohan, "India as a Security Provider: Reconsidering the Raj Legacy" (working paper, Institute of South Asian Studies, National University of Singapore, March 2012), emphasis added.

277. David Scott, "The Indo-Pacific in U.S. Strategy: Responding to Power Shifts," *Rising Powers Quarterly* 3, no. 2 (2018).

278. Scott, "The Indo-Pacific in U.S. Strategy."

279. Alex Wong, "The Indo-Pacific Strategy" (speech, East Asian and Pacific Affairs Bureau, State Department, April 2018), quoted in Scott, "The Indo-Pacific in U.S. Strategy."

280. The following draws on our earlier study, *Global Power, Client State: India's Place in the U.S. Strategic Order*, 2005. The relevant passage can be found in "Why the US Promotes India's Great-Power Ambitions," *Research Unit for Political Economy* 41 (2005).

281. Juli A. MacDonald, *Indo-U.S. Military Relationship: Expectations and Perceptions* (Falls Church, VA: Information Assurance Technology Analysis Center, 2002), 91.

282. Stephen J. Blank, *Natural Allies? Regional Security in Asia and Prospects*

for Indo-American Strategic Cooperation (Carlisle, PA: Strategic Studies Institute, U.S. Army War College, 2005), 13.

283. Blank, *Natural Allies?*, 1.
284. John Cherian, "U.S. and India: Strengthening Ties," *Frontline*, January 17, 2020.
285. Cherian, "U.S. and India."
286. Sandeep Unnithan, "Modi-Morrison Summit: How Beijing's Belligerence Makes the 'Quad' More Attractive for New Delhi," *daily O*, June 15, 2020.
287. Ankit Panda, "U.S. Navy Ship Replenishes Indian Navy Ship in South China Sea," *Diplomat*, November 6, 2019.
288. Saurabh Todi, "India Gets Serious About the Indo-Pacific," *Diplomat*, December 18, 2019.
289. Todi, "India Gets Serious About the Indo-Pacific."
290. Blank, *Natural Allies?*, 79.
291. Maria Abi-Habib, "Will India Side with the West Against China? A Test Is at Hand," *New York Times*, June 19, 2020.
292. "Poverty & Equity Brief: South Asia, India, April 2020," World Bank, April 2020.
293. Sanjay Reddy, presentation in "Smackdown Debate: How Credible Are the World Bank's Global Poverty Estimates? How Can They Be Improved?," World Bank, March 5, 2019.
294. *COVID-19 Livelihoods Survey: Compilation of Findings.*
295. "Compilation of COVID19 Lockdown Impact Surveys."
296. Research Unit for Political Economy, introduction to "India's Working Class and Its Prospects," *Aspects of India's Economy* 70 and 71 (April 2018), available at rupe-india.org.
297. Asura, "We Need to Consider Nationalising Private Hospitals If We Are to Avoid a Total Disaster," *The Wire*, July 9, 2020.
298. Rema Nagarajan, "Delhi Yet to Regulate COVID-19 Treatment Fees in Private Hospitals," *Times of India*, June 13, 2020.
299. The most glaring instance of this is the case of India's nine hundred thousand community health workers, termed "accredited social health activists," who go house to house to counsel people, monitor symptoms, and collect essential health data. Even during the COVID-19 crisis, when their workload and the risks faced have risen steeply, they are paid a derisory monthly sum of between ₹1,000 to ₹2,000, or $13 and $26, and they do not receive personal protective gear such as masks and hand sanitizer.
300. Harry Magdoff, "Economic Myths and Imperialism," *Monthly Review* 23, no. 7 (December 1971), 1.